Crescat Graffiti, Vita Excolatur: Confessions of the University of Chicago

Quinn Dombrowski

Dedicated to Robert Maynard Hutchins, whose abolishment of football left an impression on me as a prospective student.

THE   U O'C

A giant refrigerator

for nerd storage

Table of Contents

ΛΦΣ

-Are you
serious?

Introduction

The Regenstein Library has historically been at the heart of the University of Chicago social scene. As then-provost Richard Saller told the Chicago Tribune in 2005, "On our campus, it's not the football game that draws the biggest crowd, it's evening study in the library."[1]

Students socialize underground on the A-level until dawn, spilling their joys, anguish, and problem sets onto the whiteboards that line the walls of the group study areas. For those who prefer solitude, the reading rooms are filled with cubicles whose occupants glare at anyone who dares to break the silence through coughs or flip-flops. To escape human contact altogether, one can retreat to the study nooks in the stacks. In these isolated spaces, silent conversations spread across the walls, building upon and refuting one another until their expansiveness leads to their demise at the hands of University facilities.

This is a selection of the 700+ pieces of graffiti documented in public study areas of the Regenstein Library between July 2007 and October 2009, though some pieces date as early as 2005. As the university administration has pointed out, this has been a time of cultural change for the College, which is reflected in the graffiti.

This book is a celebration of the shared experience of University of Chicago alumni who at some point in their college experience retreated to the library for hour after maddening hour, finishing a paper, studying for an exam, or catching up on homework.

---

[1] http://www-news.uchicago.edu/citations/05/050605.reg-ct.html

Thanks and Acknowledgments

This book would not be possible without the students who spilled their thoughts, feelings, frustrations, and doodles all over the Regenstein Library. Some of them have heard about this project and gotten in touch with me. Janice Rumschlag was asleep under the whiteboard drawing on page 86 when I took the picture in April 2008; her friend Meara Charnetzki drew it for her. Meara is also responsible for the languishing knight on page 71. Moira Cassidy drew the girl with short hair and glasses on page 126. Daniel Choi is behind three very different pieces of graffiti: "Even if you fail your classes" (p. 82), LOLCats (p. 59) and "Organic Chemistry is Voodoo Witchcraft" (p. 26). You can find the hilarious and heartwarming stories behind Daniel's pieces, as well as the most up-to-date list of graffiti artists, at http://www.crescatgraffiti.com/thanks.

Without the linguistic expertise of the following individuals, much of the multilingual graffiti would still be titled "Greek graffiti", "Chinese graffiti", etc. The Arabic was translated by alphaprivee on Flickr; the Chinese was translated by Matthew Felix Sun and Ping Lieser, the Devanagari was translated by wally.mars on Flickr, the Greek was translated by Athanassios Vérgados, the Japanese was translated by Toshi Katayama and Lane Ware, Christian Hilchey provided Latin consultation, Bihui Li made sense out of the leetspeak, and Andy Dombrowski translated the Turkish. The rest I figured out.

This project has taken over two years to complete, and there's been times when my motivation has faltered. In April 2009, Molly Ammons in Monterey, California wrote the first blog post about the Regenstein graffiti[1]. That post inspired me to get back to taking pictures in the stacks after four months of neglect. In July 2009, Carolyn Kellogg wrote a post on the L.A. Times 'Jacket Copy' blog[2] that generated a lot of interest, and, with the encouragement of Sara Ware, convinced me to put together this book. The book project had begun to languish in a state of semi-completion when, in October 2009, Marcus Gilmer wrote about the graffiti on the Chicagoist[3]. Without these gentle reminders that this was a project worth continuing, it would have remained nothing more than an unorganized, un-updated set of over 700 photos on Flickr.

[1] http://commonfates.blogspot.com/2009/04/written-on-wall.html
[2] http://latimesblogs.latimes.com/jacketcopy/2009/07/library-graffiti-at-the-university-of-chicago.html
[3] http://chicagoist.com/2009/10/16/graffiti_gallery.php

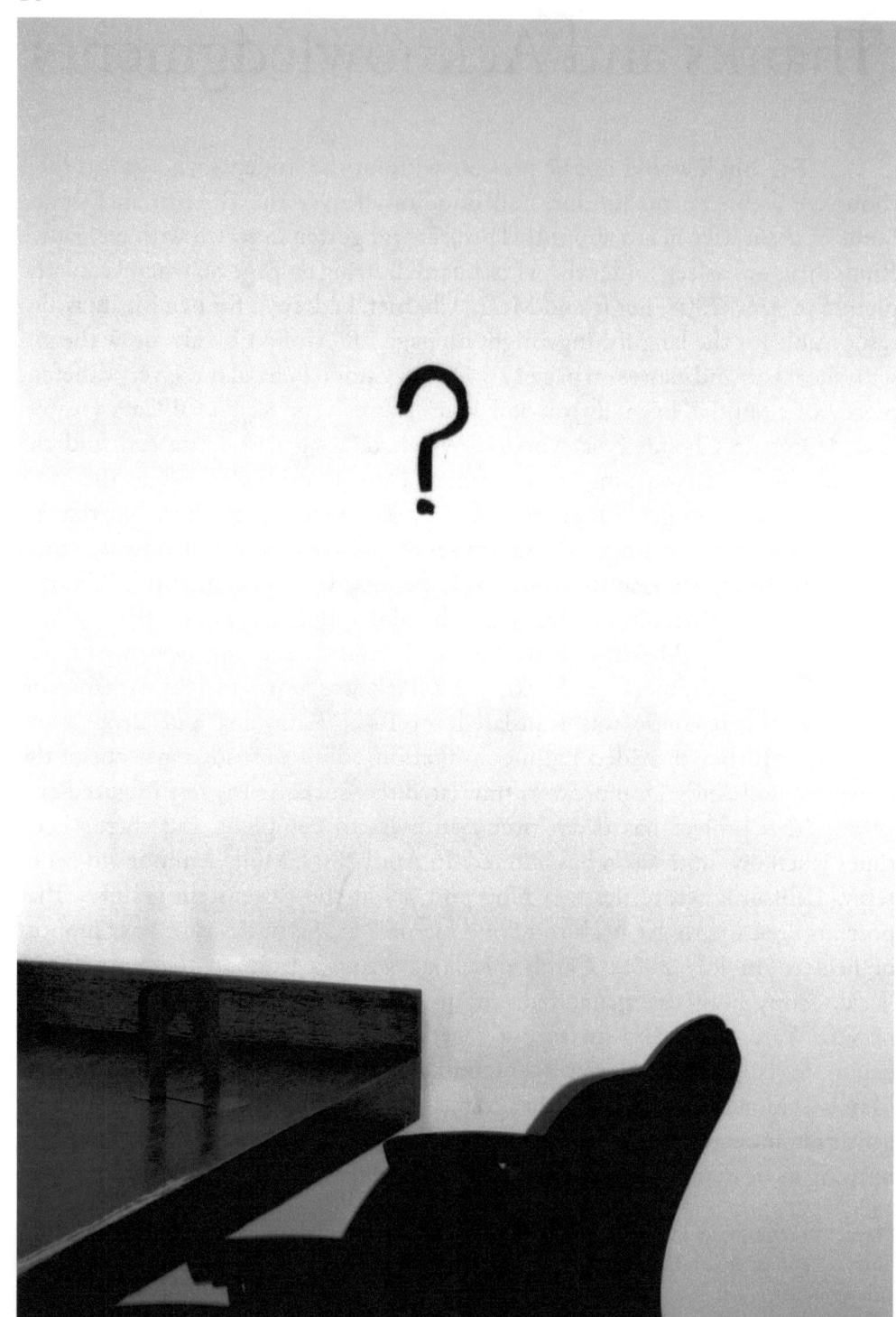

Logic

$Gay^2 + travis^2 = Marshall (straight)$ a.k.a. (NO! HOMO!)

$travis^2 = my\ new\ haircut!$ $\sqrt{dan}$ $= Gay$

$\therefore Dan = Gay^2$ (that's really gay)

1. $WOMAN = TIME \times MONEY$
2. $TIME\ is\ MONEY : TIME = MONEY$ (A+)
3. $WOMAN = MONEY^2$

All I wanna do is...

4. Money is the Root of all problems.

$MONEY = \sqrt{problems} \rightarrow MONEY^2 = problems$

fuck a DOG in THE ASS

AND, AS DEFINED IN 3,

$WOMAN = Problems.$

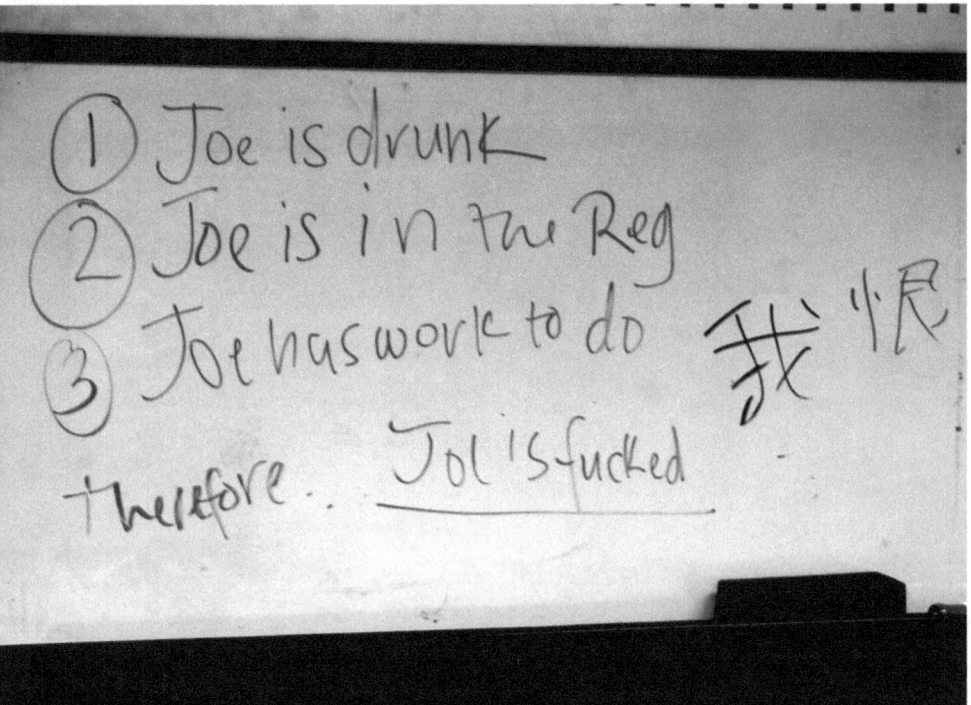

① Joe is drunk
② Joe is in the Reg
③ Joe has work to do 我 恨

therefore.. Joe's fucked

what is logic?
everything I do.
who defines reason? ME.
my quest has taken me
through the physical, metaphysical
and back.

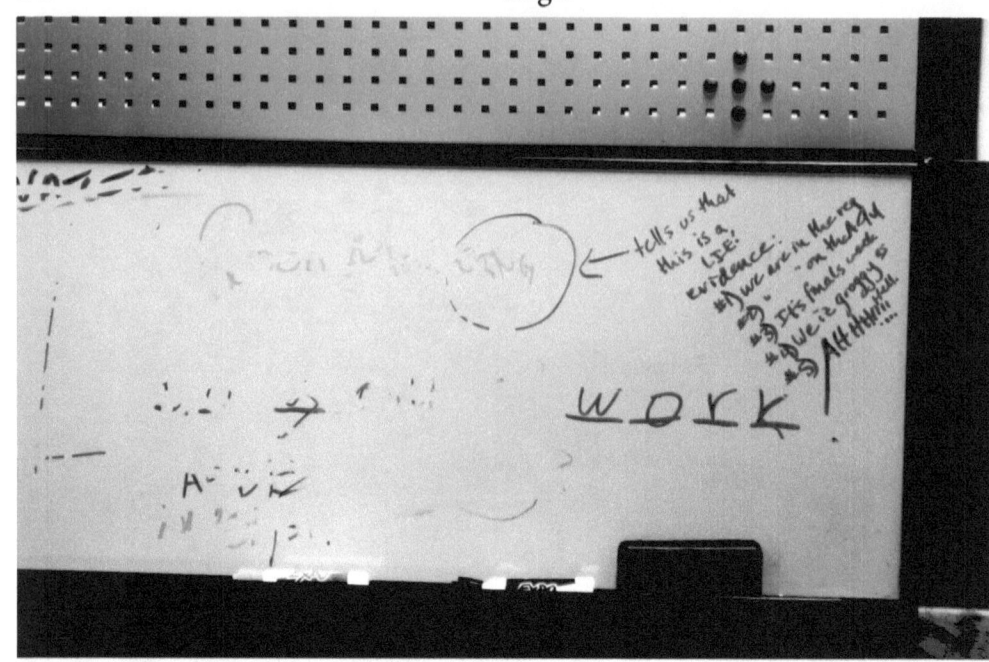

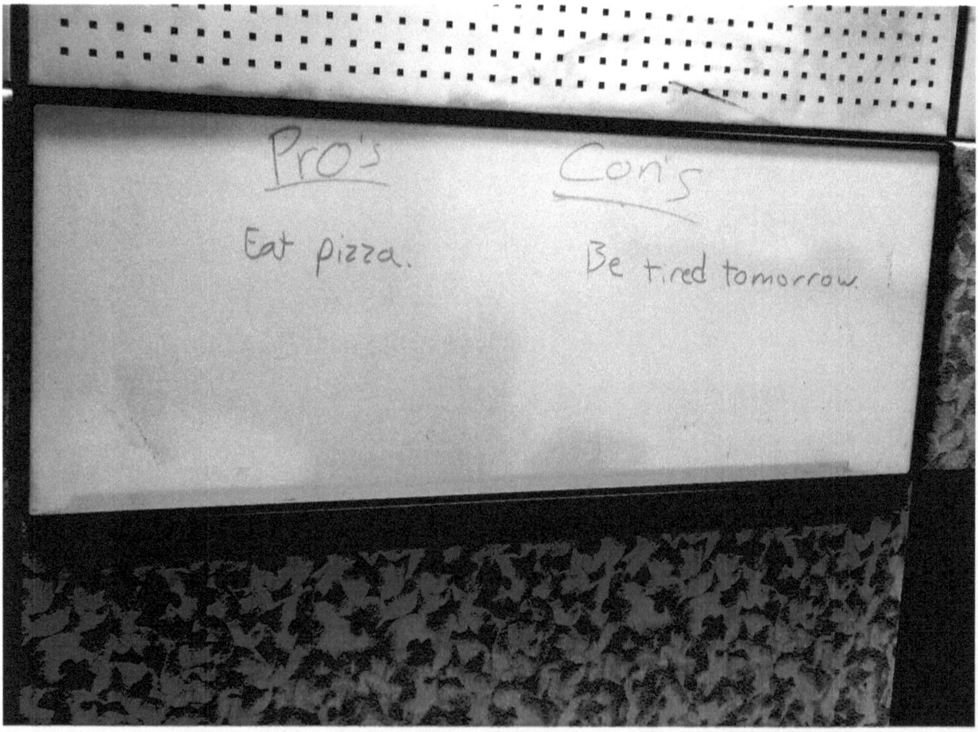

Advice

Go to Italy.
        Be a cobbler.

" If you're a lawyer in, like, Indonesia,
and you come here, no one's going to
want you to tell them the best
way to bribe Suharto. "

$P(\underline{rbrrb})$

$r_1 b_2 r_3 r_2 b,$

$5! = \dfrac{3! \cdot 2!}{5!}$

$r \, b \, r \, r \, b$

let your passions
incinerate themselves
and in their ashes
you may find silence

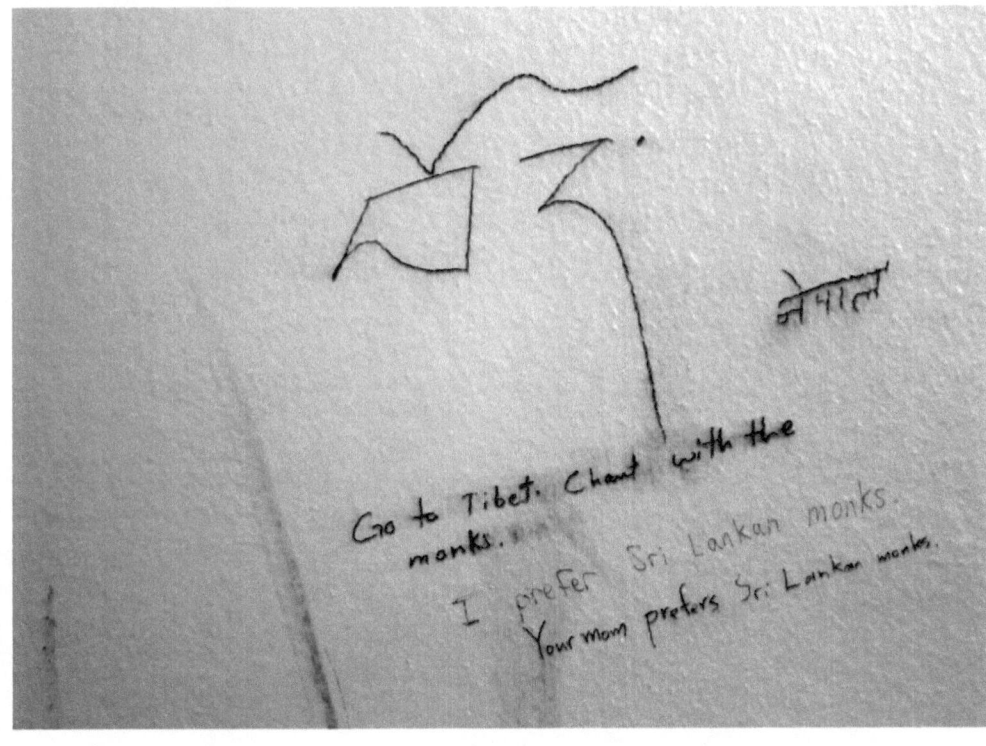

नेपाल

Go to Tibet. Chant with the
monks.
I prefer Sri Lankan monks.
Your mom prefers Sri Lankan monks.

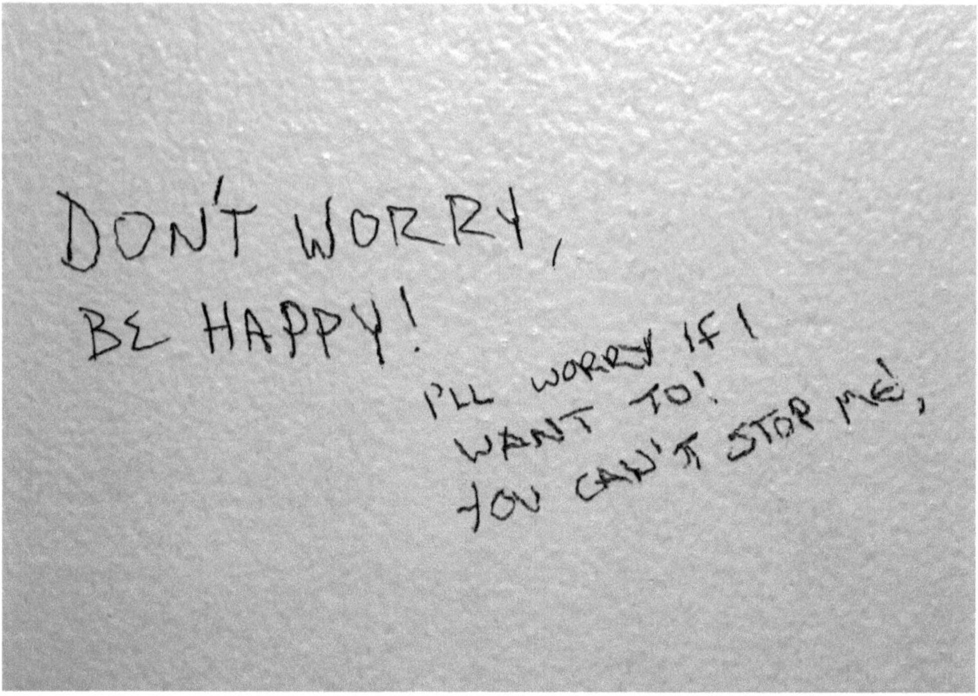
DON'T WORRY,
BE HAPPY!
I'LL WORRY IF I
WANT TO!
YOU CAN'T STOP ME!

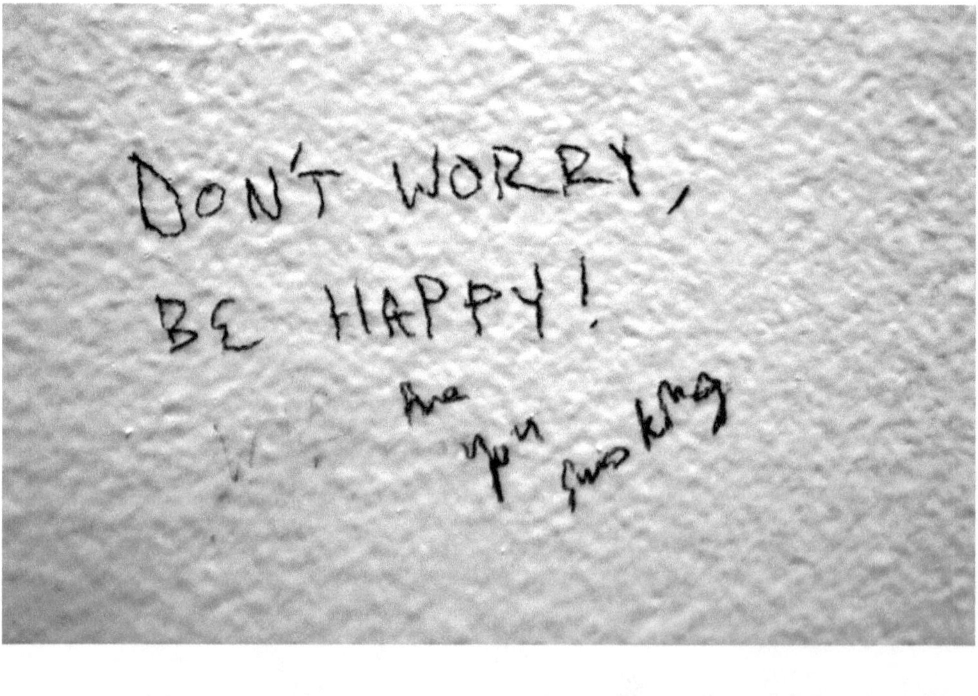
DON'T WORRY,
BE HAPPY!
Are
you
smoking

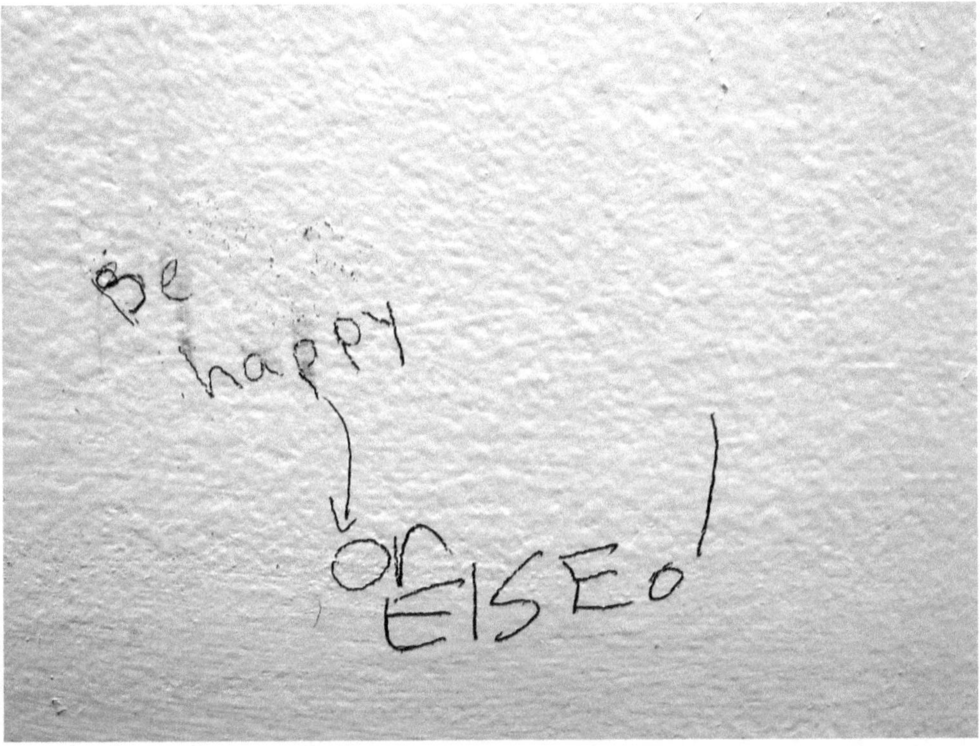

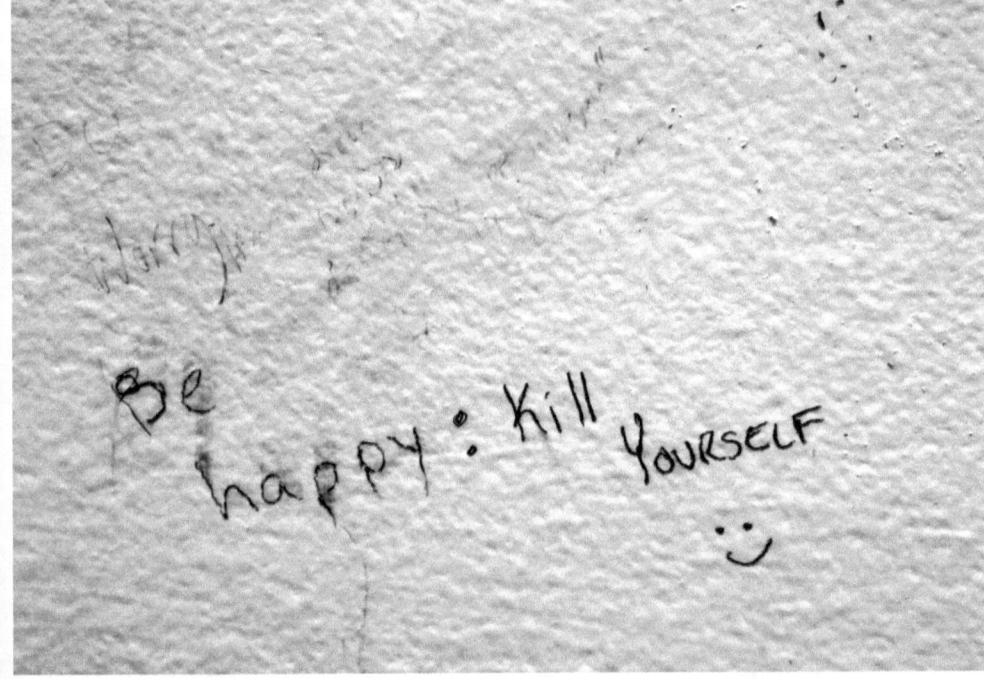

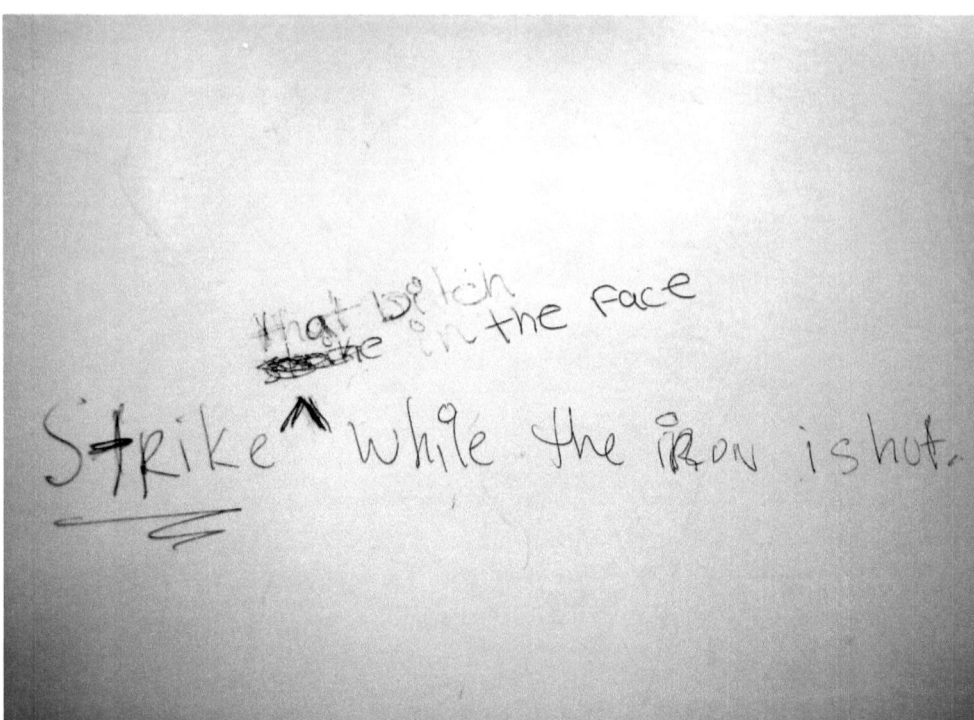

Be happy, love life, make friends, votes for women!

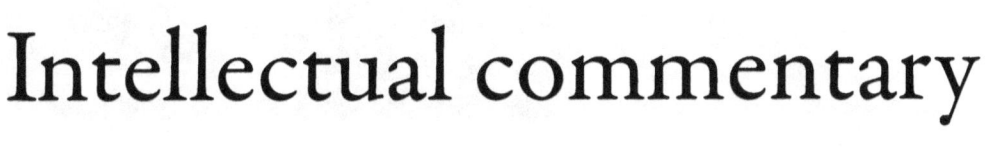

Intellectual commentary

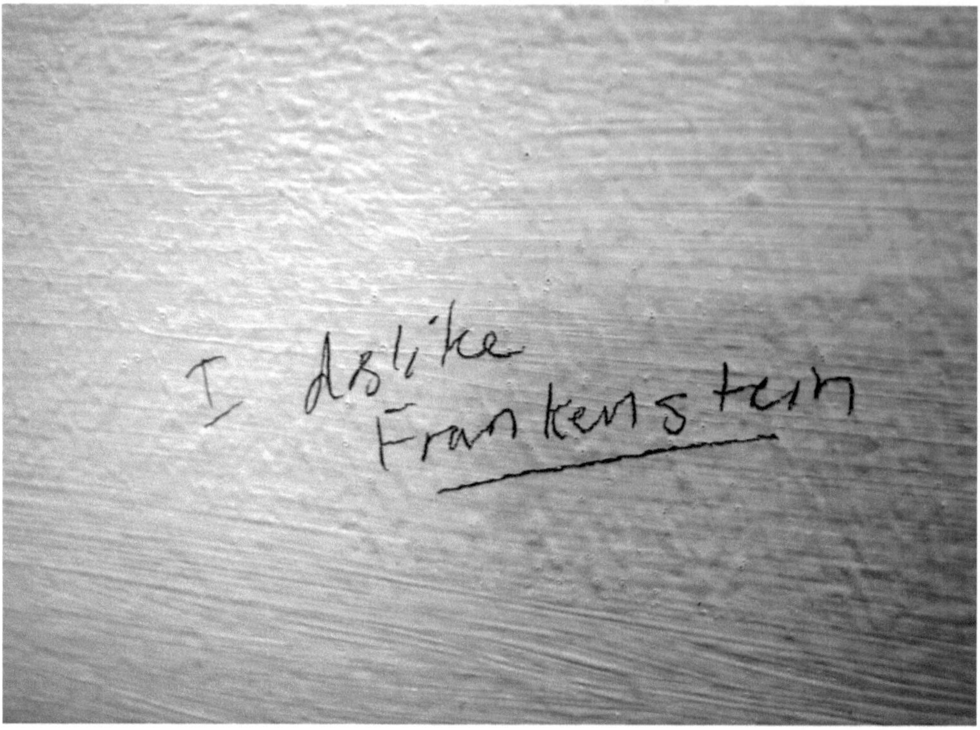
I dislike
Frankenstein

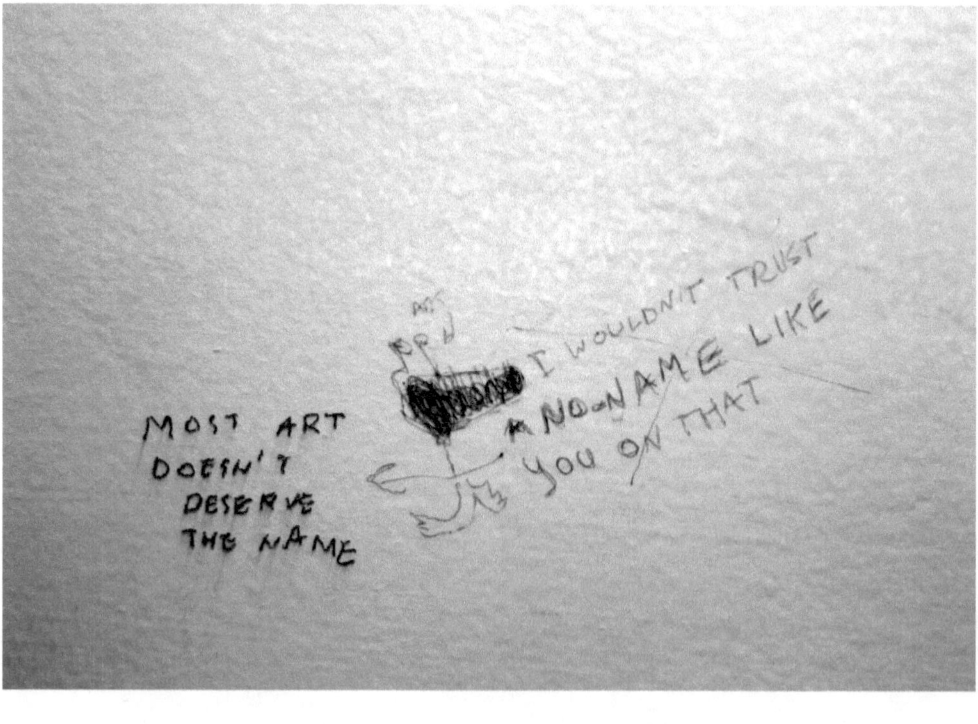
MOST ART
DOESN'T
DESERVE
THE NAME
I WOULDN'T TRUST
A NO-NAME LIKE
YOU ON THAT

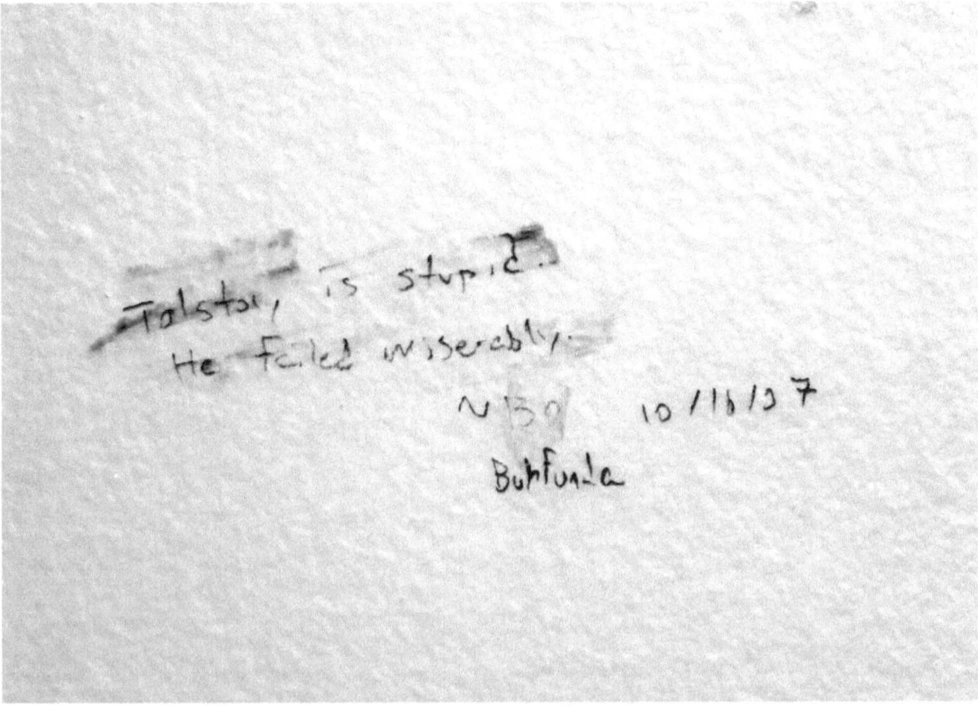
Tolstoy is stupid.
He failed miserably.

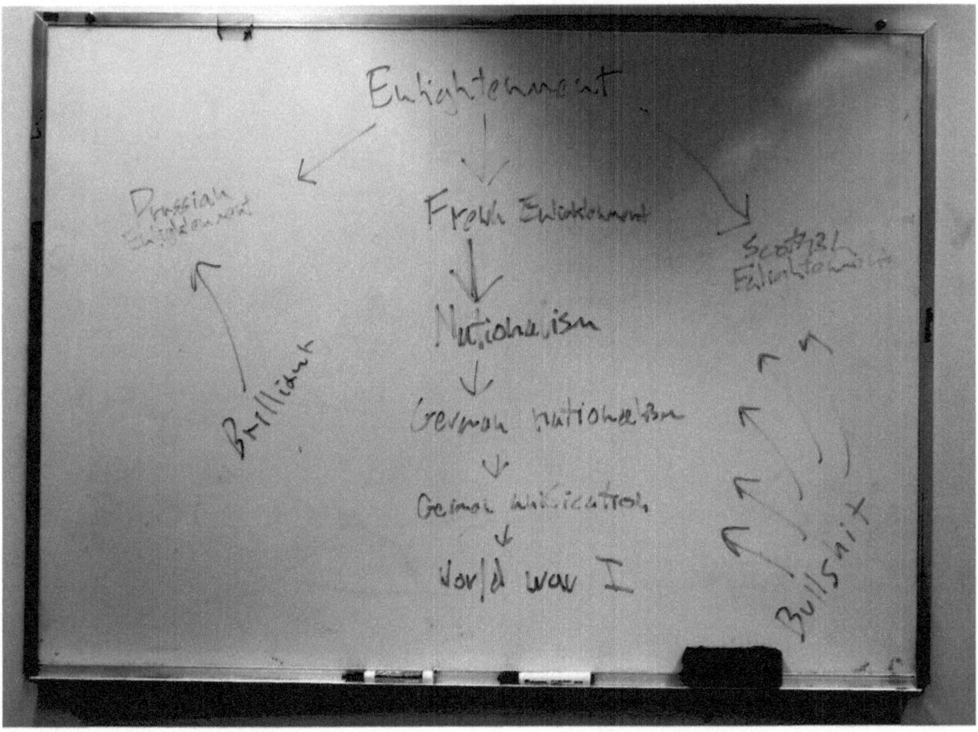
Enlightenment
Prussian Enlightenment
French Enlightenment
Scottish Enlightenment
Nationalism
German nationalism
German unification
World war I
Brilliant
Bullshit

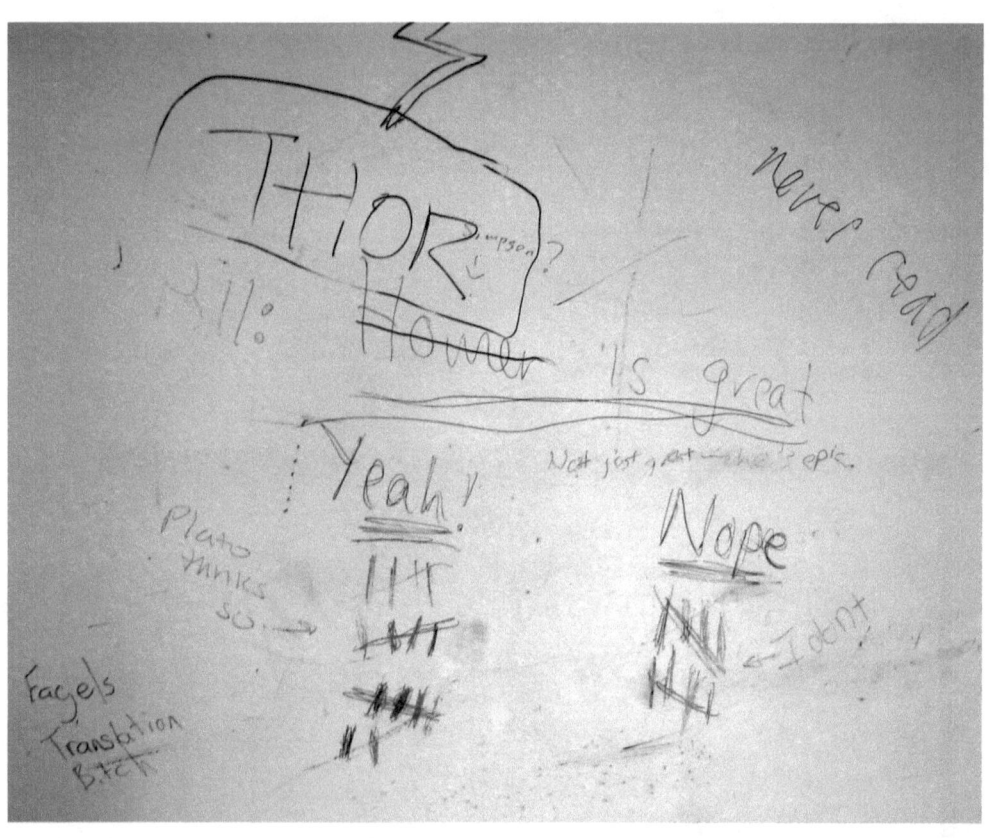

Chemistry

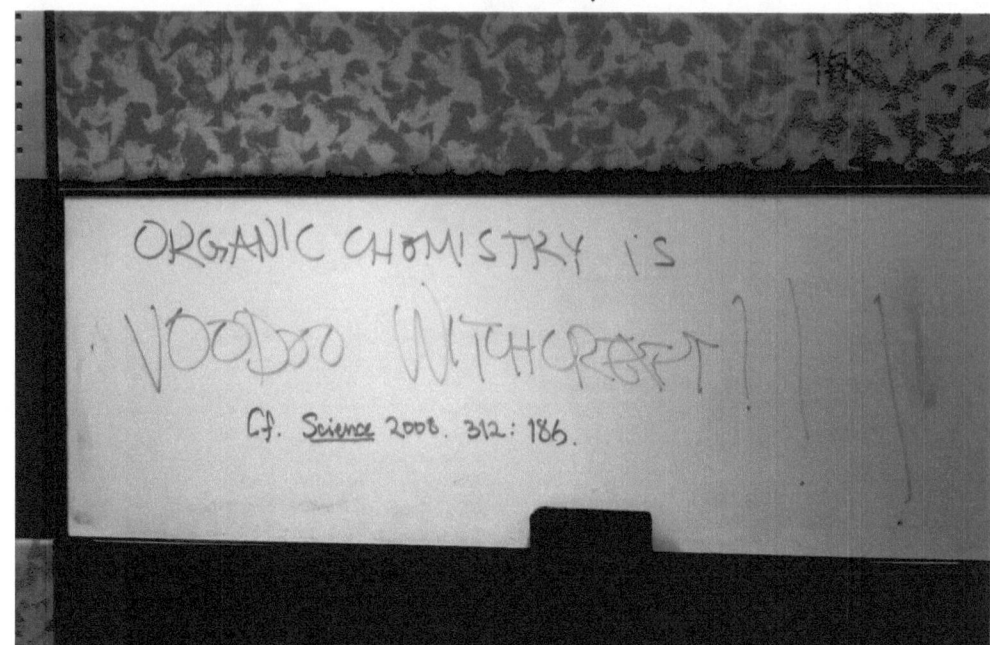

ORGANIC CHEMISTRY IS

VOODOO WITCHCRAFT?

Cf. *Science* 2006. 312: 186.

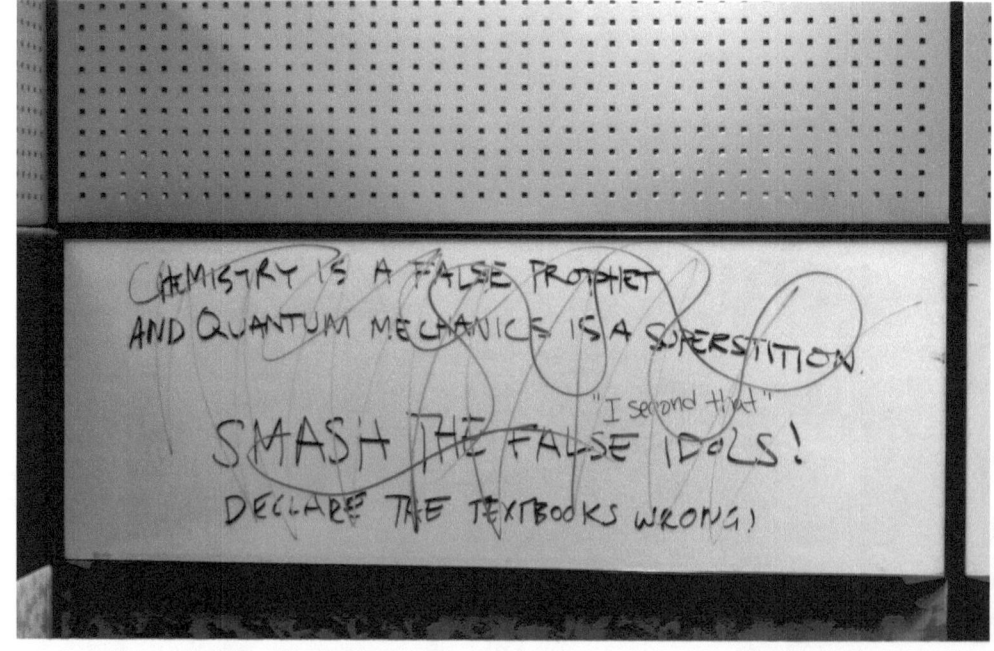

CHEMISTRY IS A FALSE PROPHET
AND QUANTUM MECHANICS IS A SUPERSTITION.

"I second that"

SMASH THE FALSE IDOLS!

DECLARE THE TEXTBOOKS WRONG!

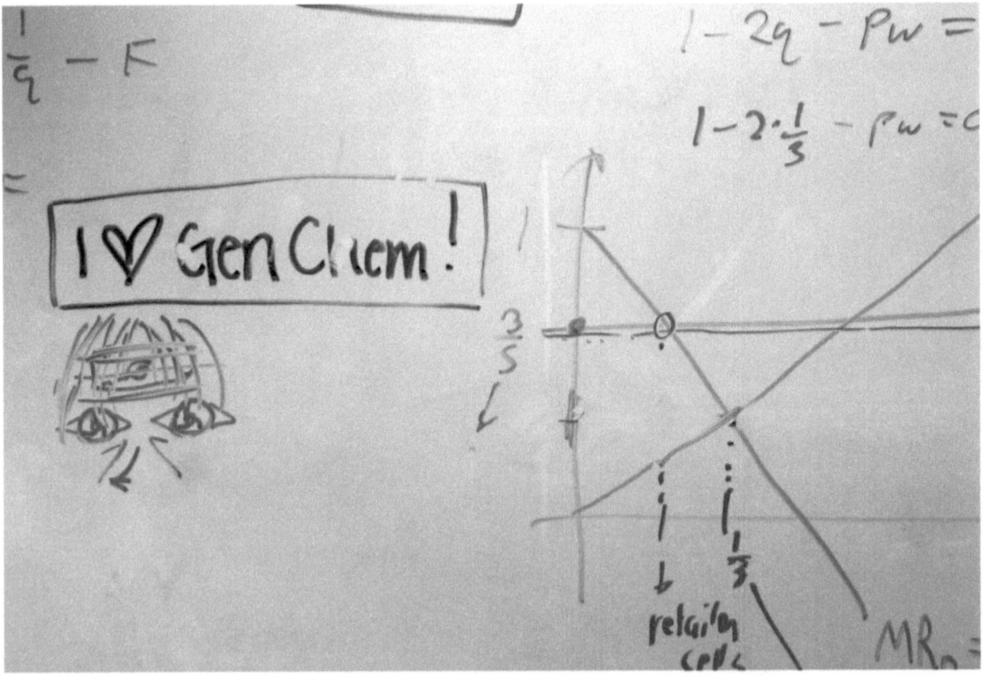

$$\frac{1}{q} - K$$

$$=$$

$$1 - 2q - Pw =$$

$$1 - 2 \cdot \frac{1}{3} - Pw = c$$

I ♥ Gen Chem !

$$\frac{3}{5}$$

$$\frac{1}{3}$$

retailer cells

$$MR_n =$$

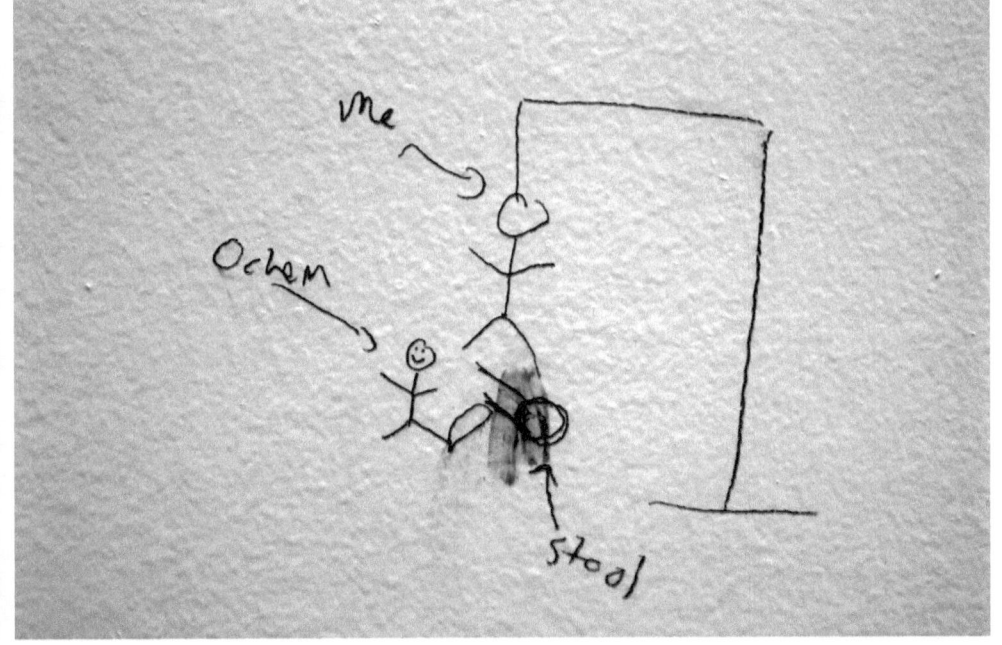

me

Ochem

stool

O-Chem is
hell on
earth!!

~~f*@~~ up. ← but it is
grow   "grow some
                         gender theory!"

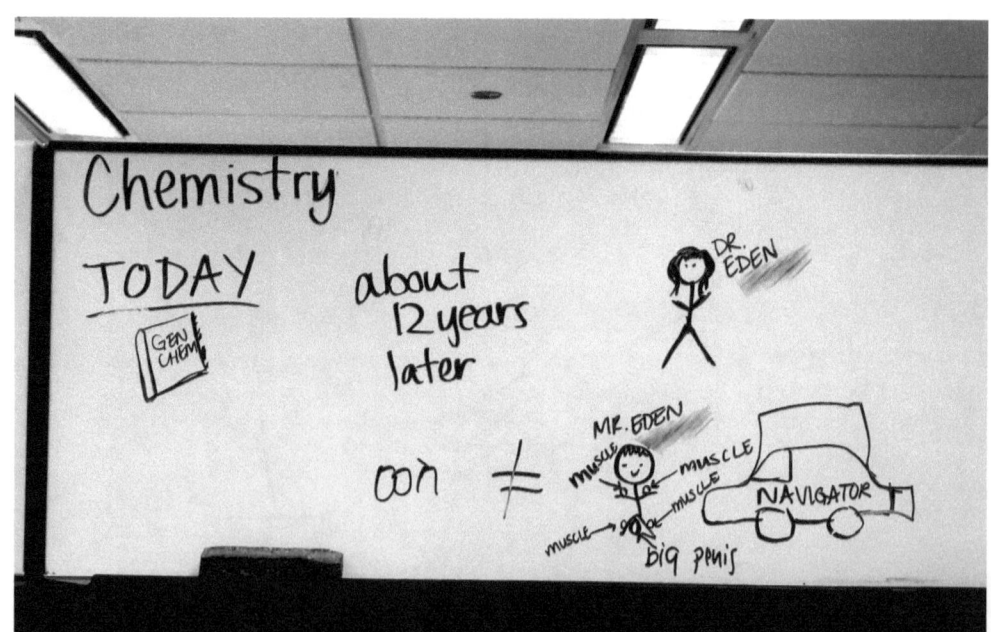

Chemistry

TODAY
[GEN CHEM ✓]

about
12 years
later

DR. EDEN

oon ≠ MR. EDEN
            muscle MUSCLE
            muscle MUSCLE
            big penis   NAVIGATOR

Love

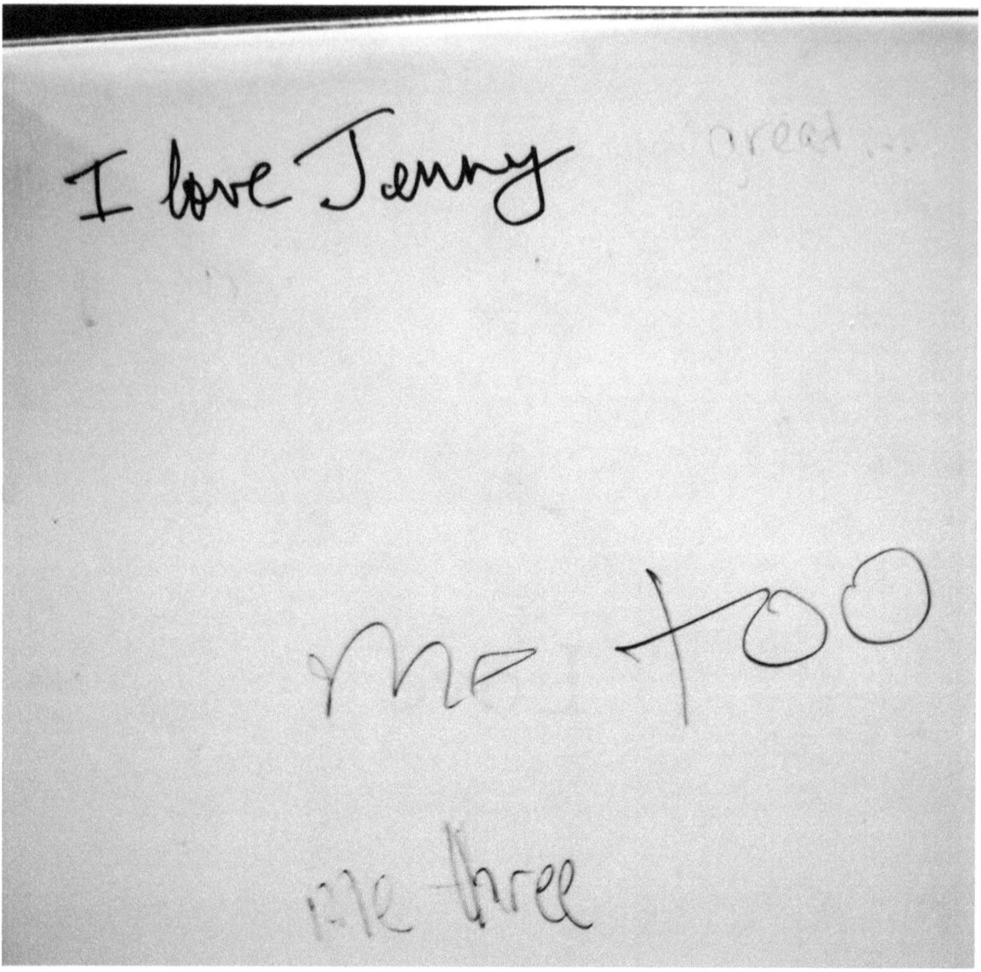
I love Jenny
great...
me too
me three

WILL YOU BE MY GIRLFRIEND?

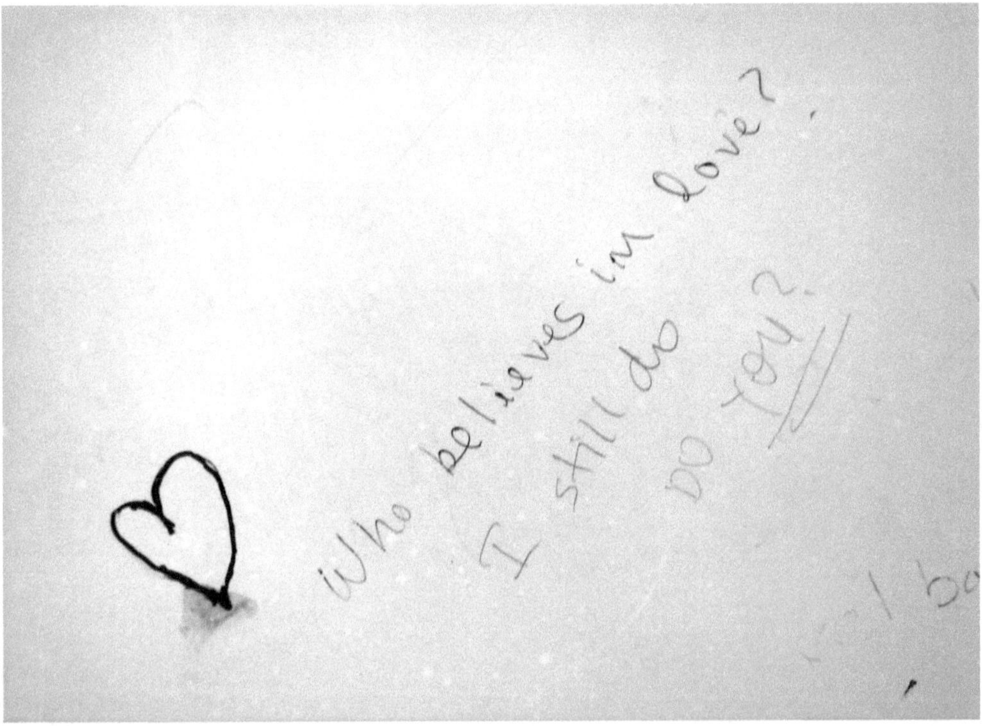

Who believes in love?
I still do
DO YOU?

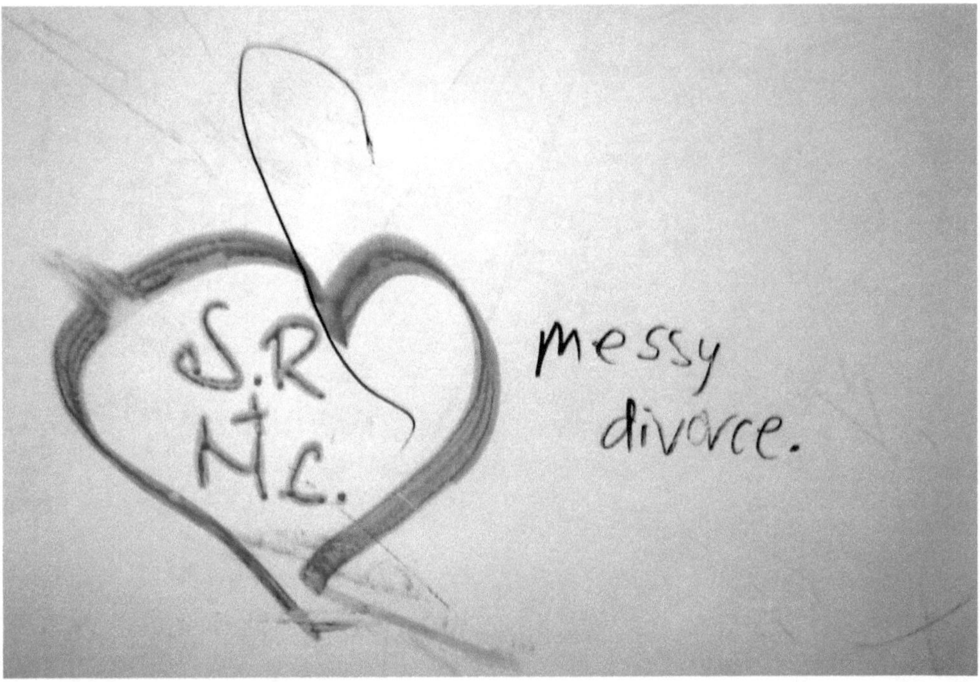

S.R
M.C.

messy divorce.

I'm lonely. not sad. just lonely.

I'm cute ; yes (smart but lonely.

Its
because
you're
a bitch

all I ever learned from love
is how to shoot
somebody who out drew you

How do you
know when
you're in love?

love is a ...   someone's
                      a little
                      bitter :)

Bastard child of guilt and shame **and Benjamin's mother**

I heard from someone you're still pretty

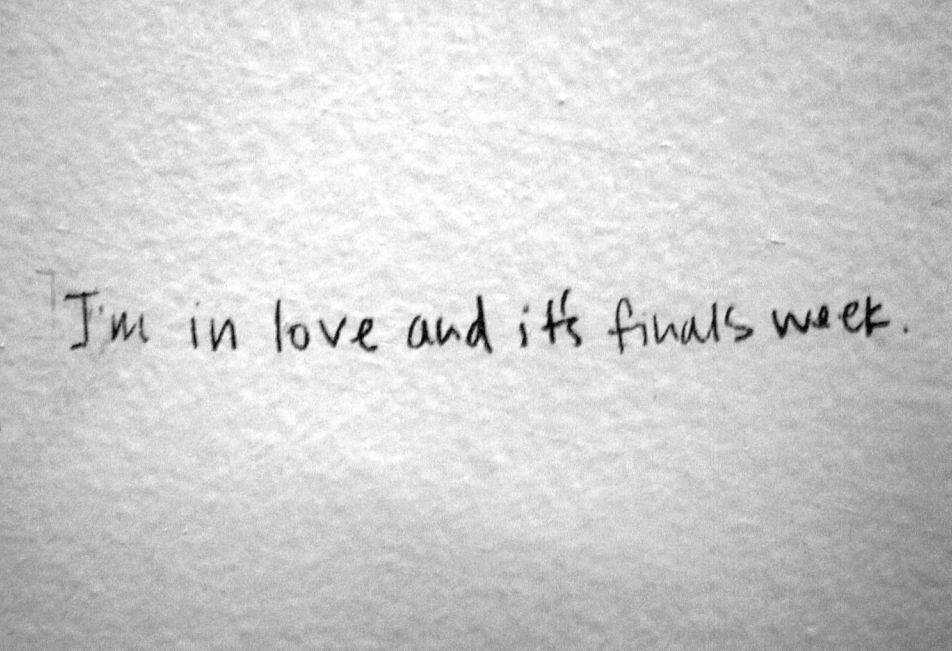

I'm in love and it's finals week.

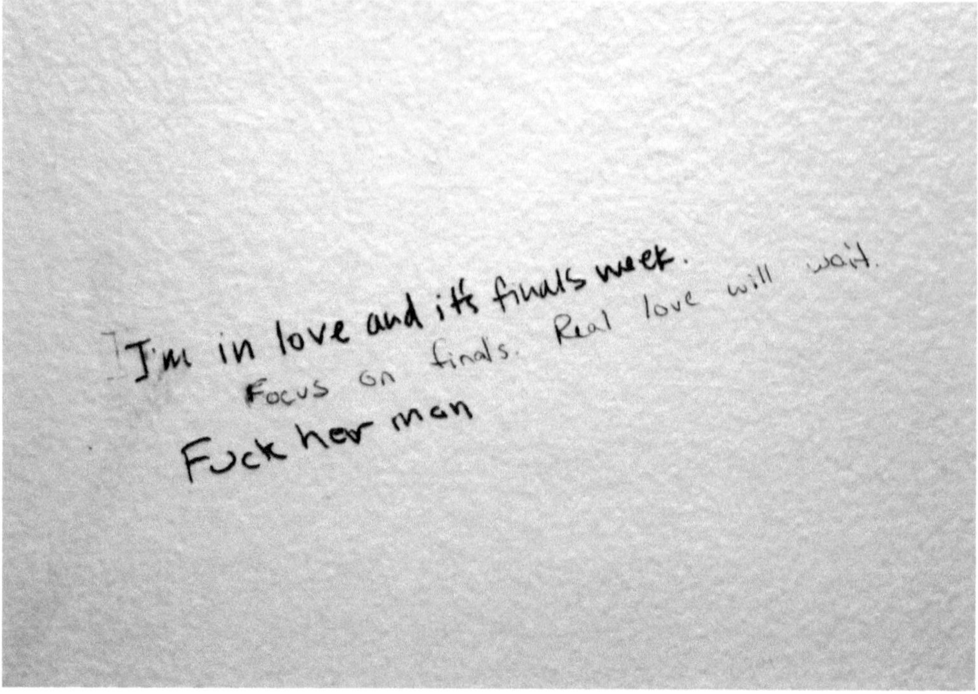

I'm in love and its finals week.
Focus on finals. Real love will wait.
Fuck her man

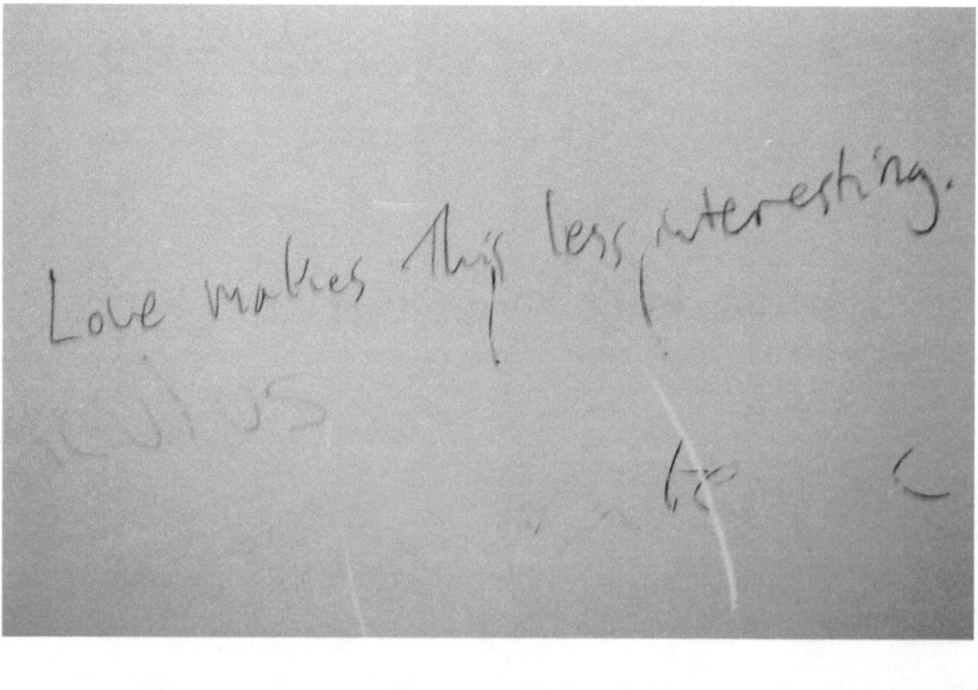

Love makes this less interesting.

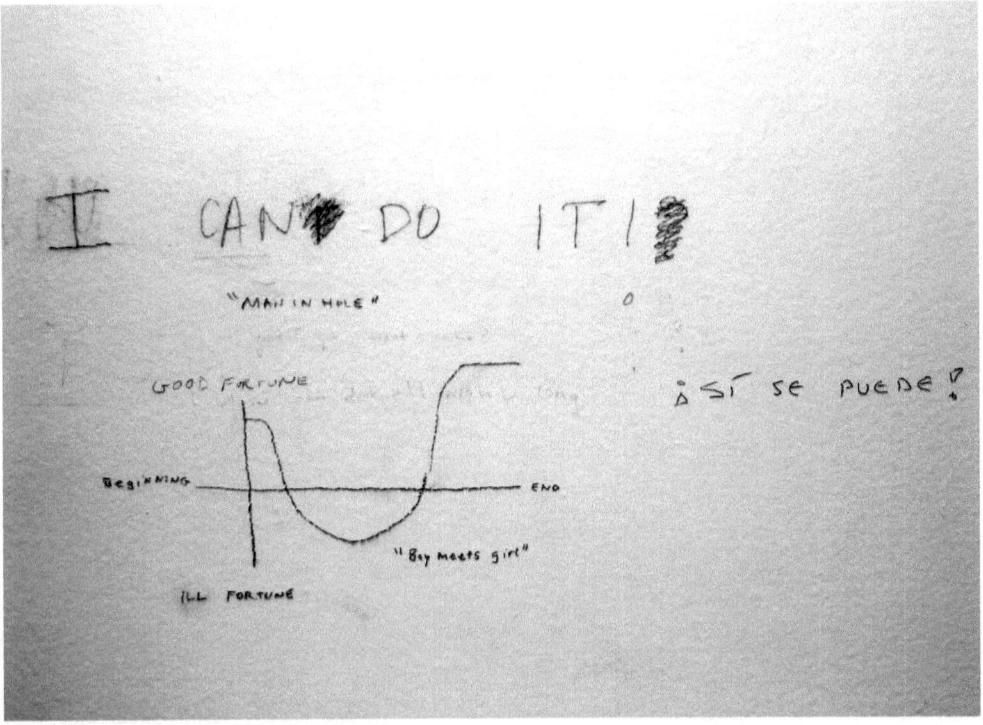

I CAN̶ DO IT!

"MAN IN HOLE"

GOOD FORTUNE

BEGINNING — END

ILL FORTUNE

"Boy meets girl"

¿ SI SE PUEDE !

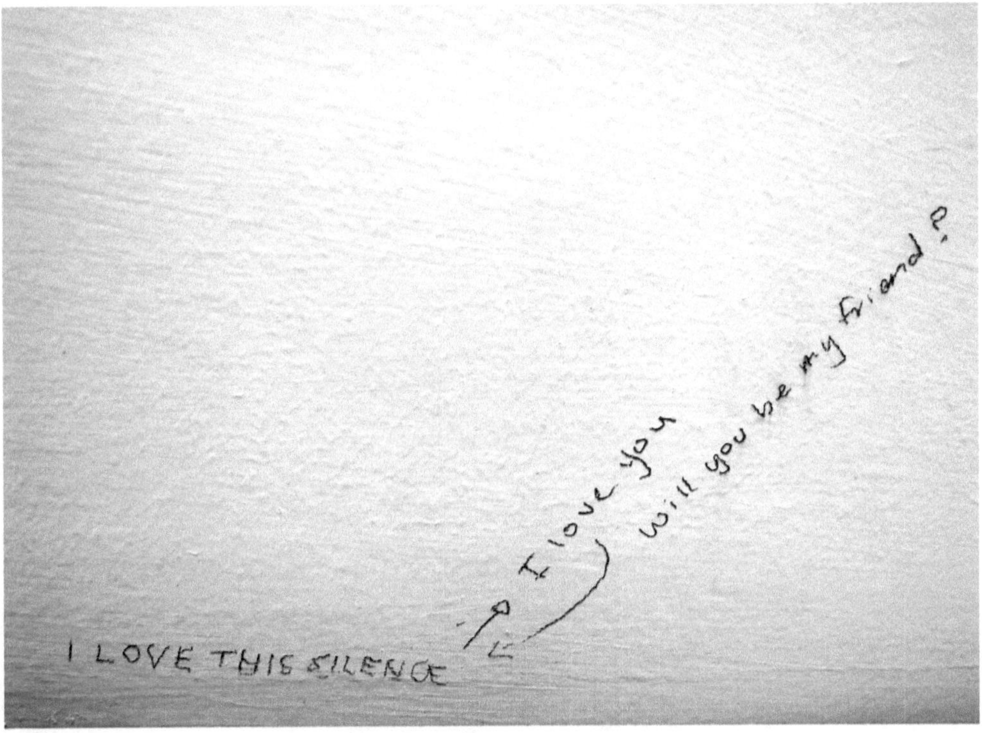

I love you

Will you be my friend ?

I LOVE THIS SILENCE

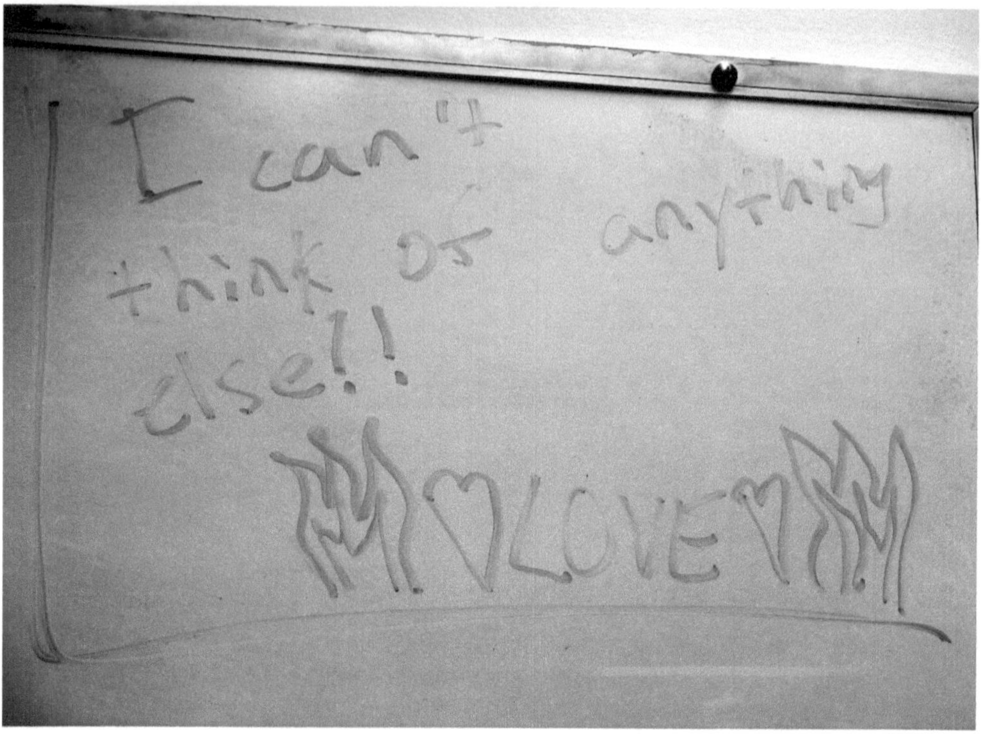

Sex

Is sex with a zombie necrophilia?

SUCK MY COCK?

NO.

PLEASE?

hmmm...

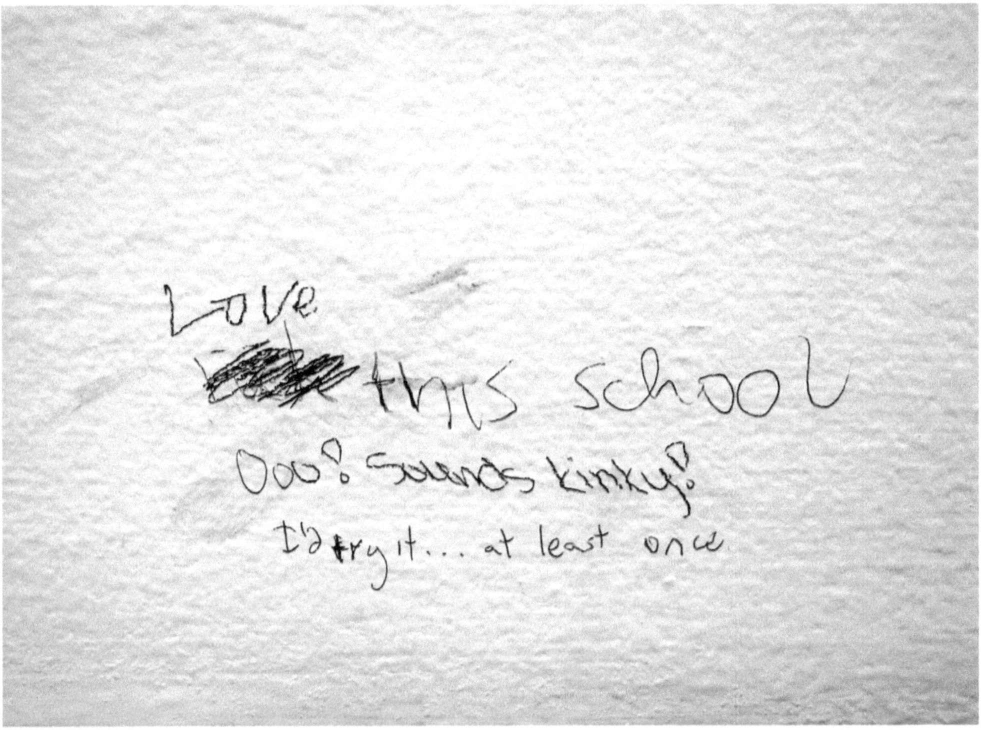

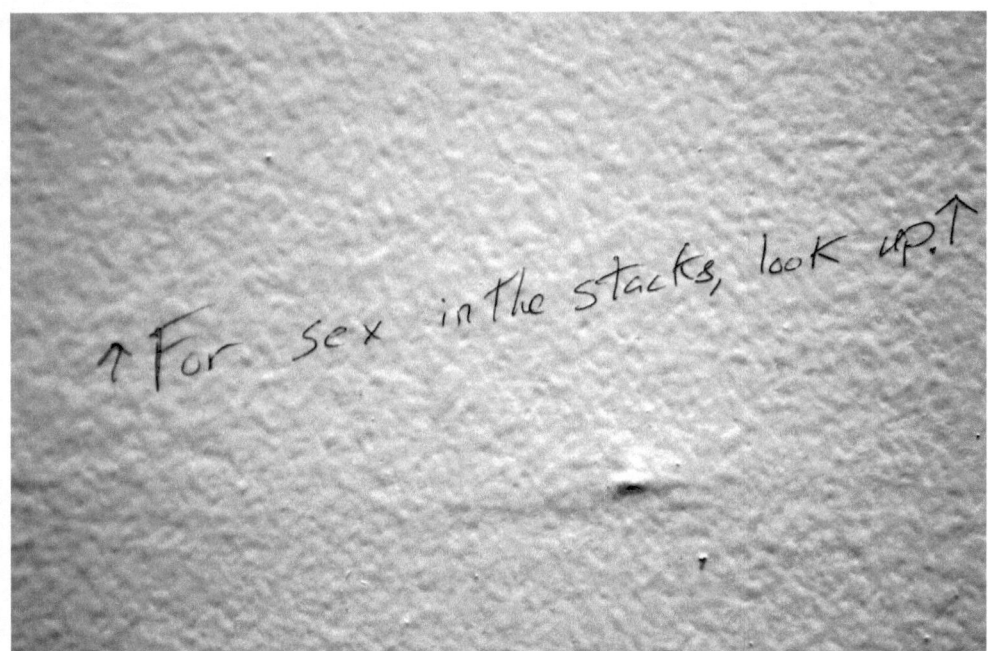

(Note: There was nothing there)

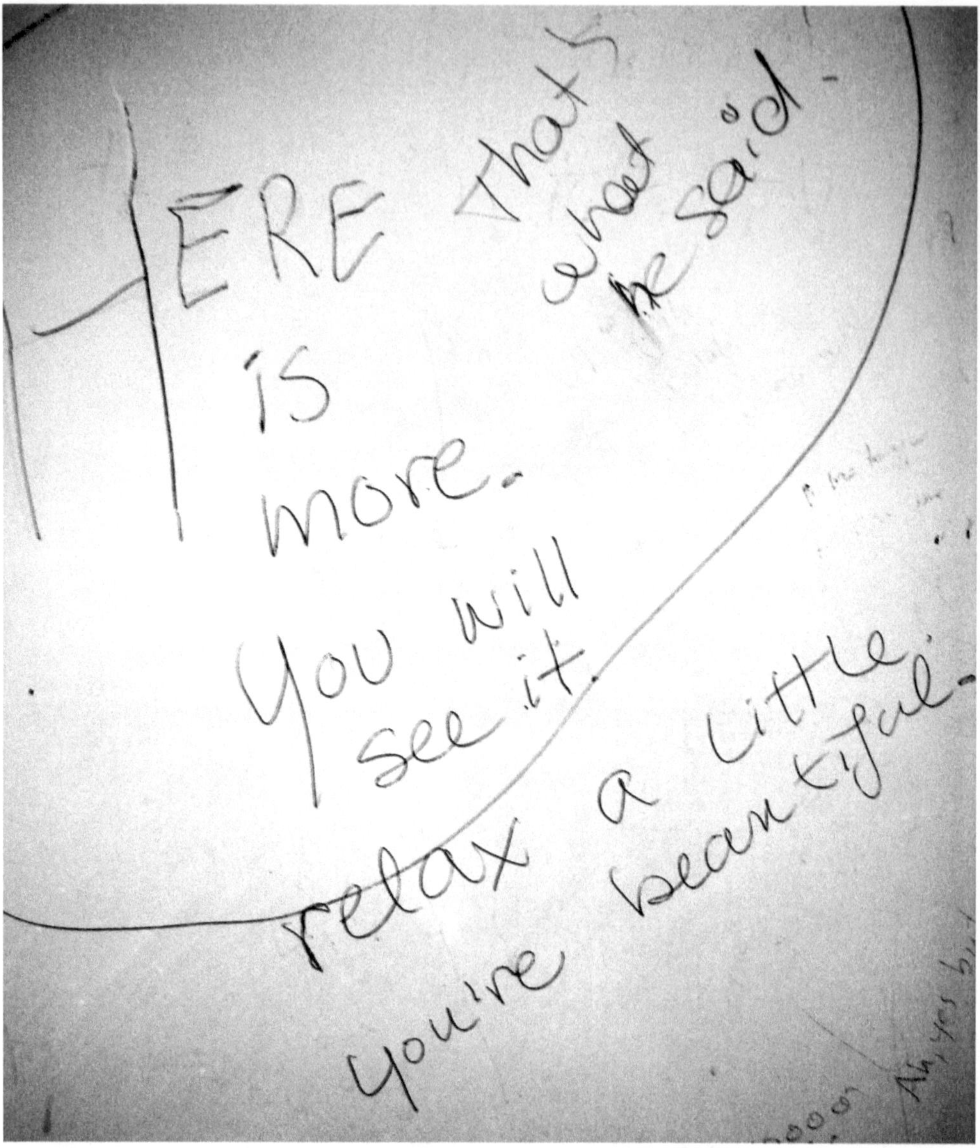

HERE is more. you will see it.

That's what he said -

relax a little you're beautiful.

Ah yes but...

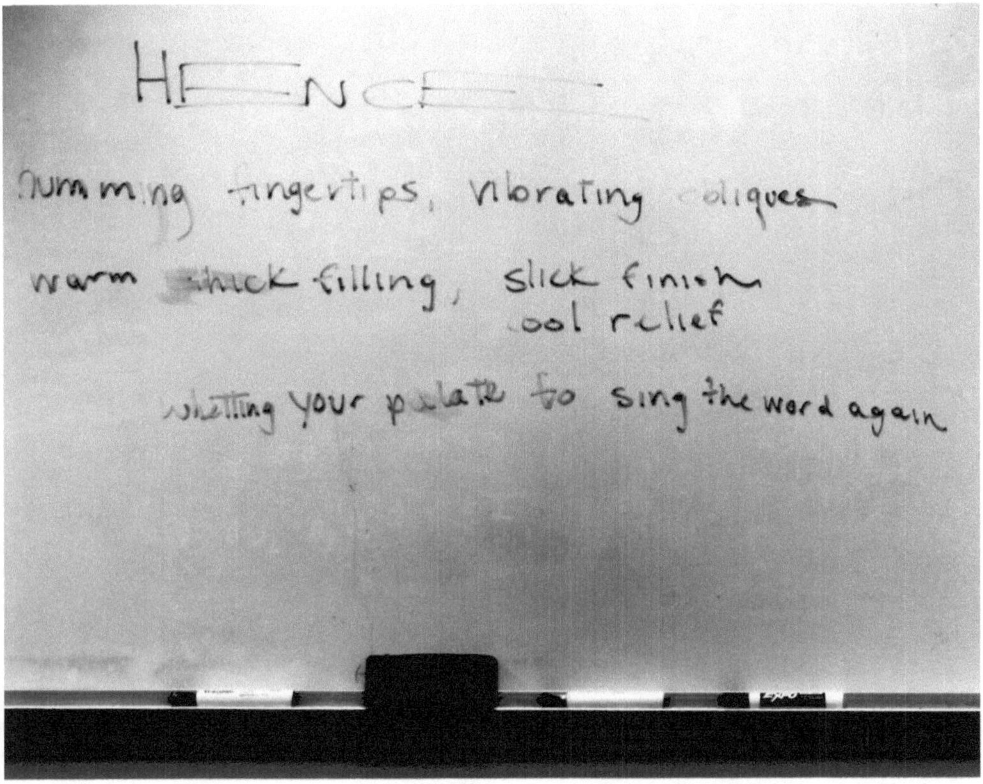

HENCE

humming fingertips, vibrating obliques

warm thick filling, slick finish
cool relief

whetting your palate to sing the word again

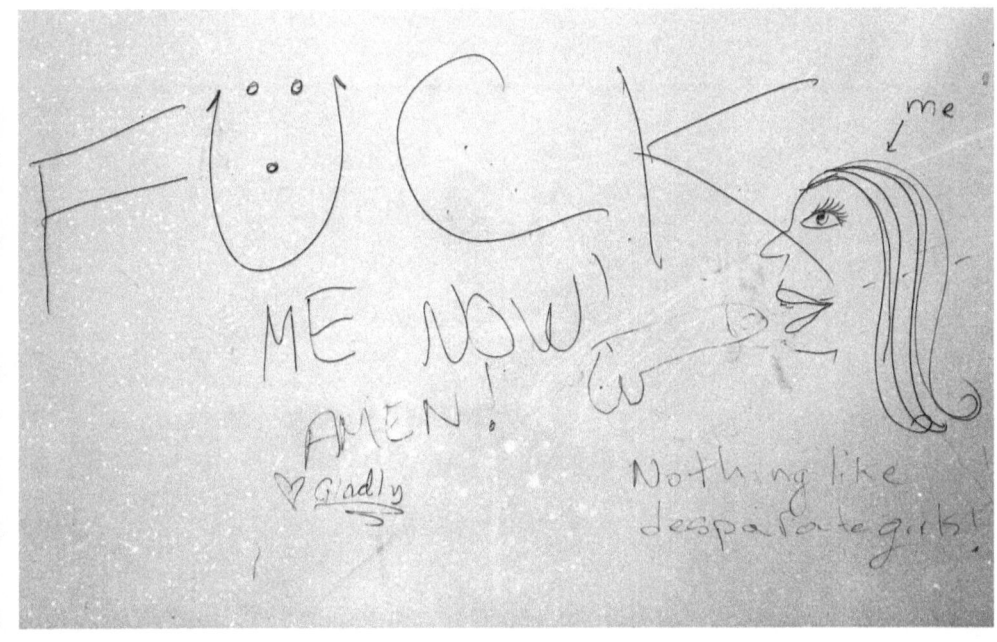

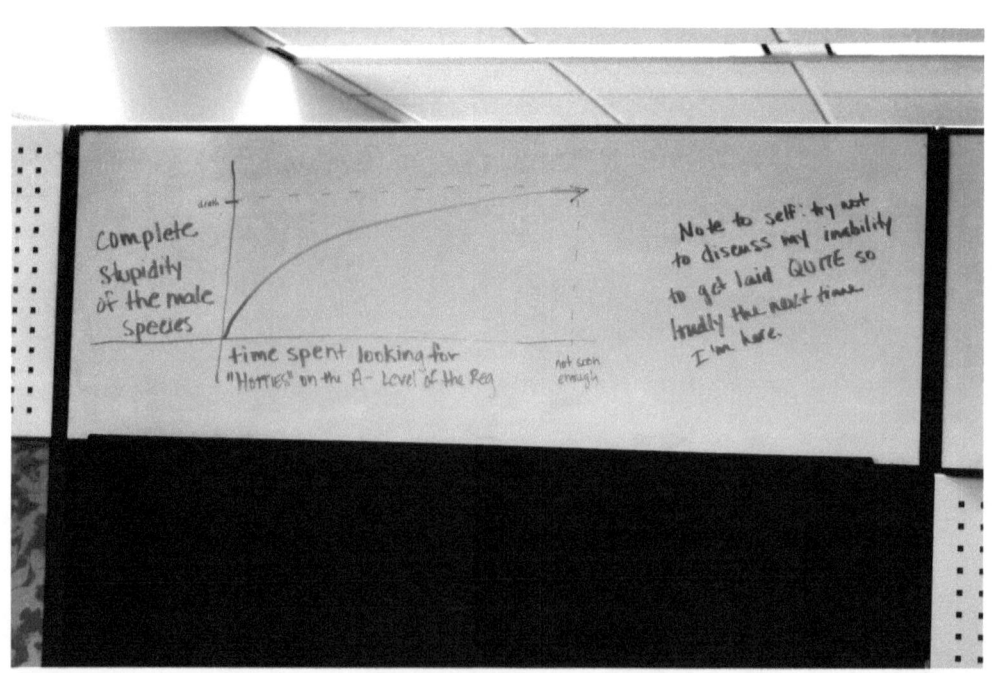

Despair

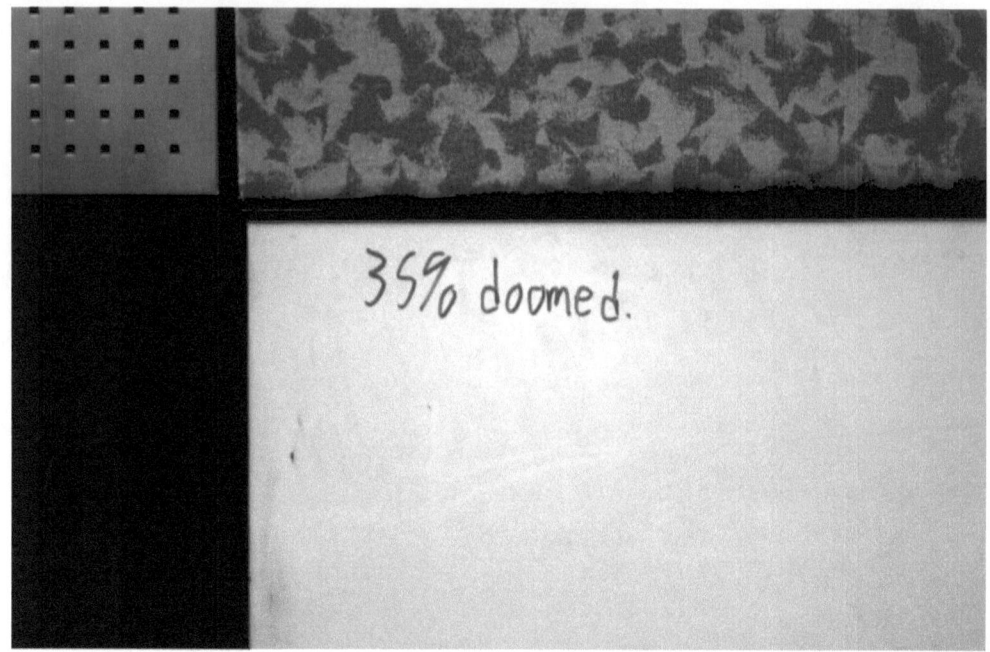

35% doomed.

there isn't enough
alcohol. in the
state of Illinois.
not for this...

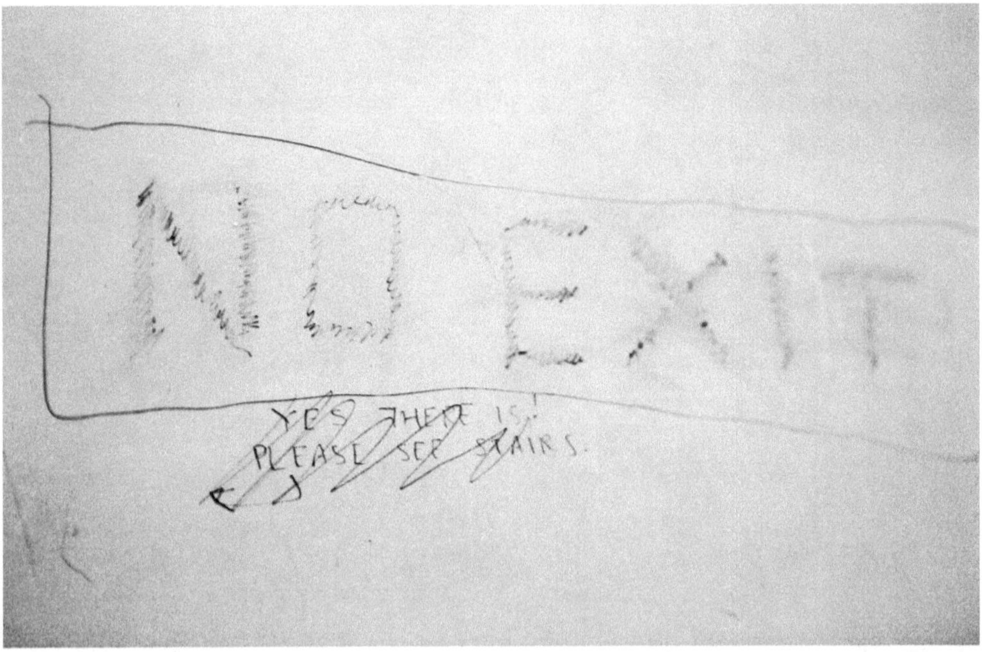
NO EXIT
YES THERE IS!
PLEASE SEE STAIRS.

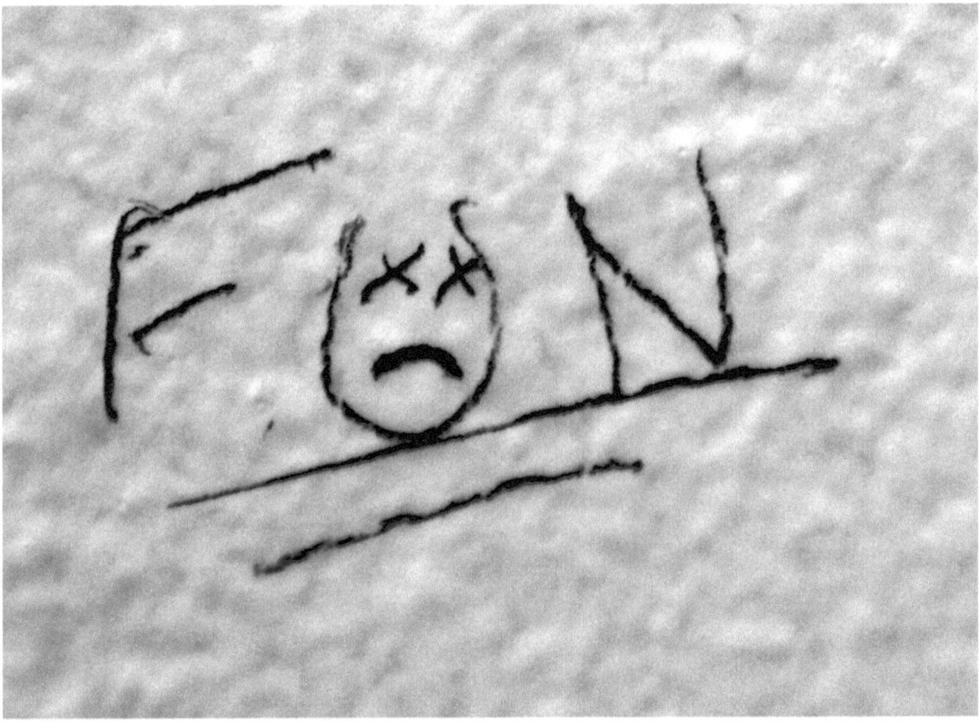

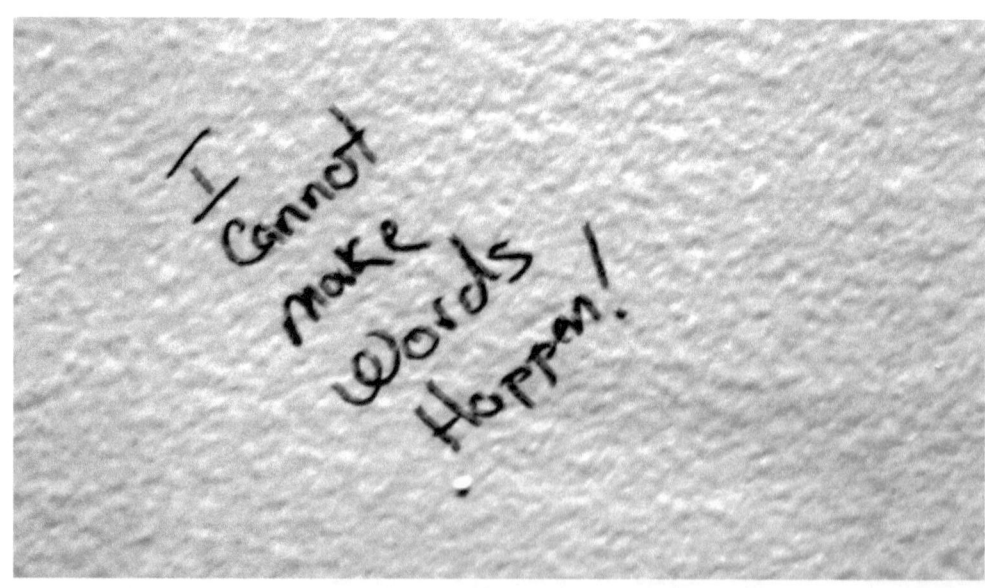

I was in a store and looking to buy
when in the corner of my eye I spied a fly
The fly looked wise and could not lie
So I made up my mind and spoke to the fly
To the fly who was wise, the fly that was wise
and could not lie, and so spoke I:
"Oh wise fly who cannot lie,
What should I buy, what should I buy?"
The wise fly sighed and looked into my eyes
he sighed in reply and I HATE MYSELF

I cannot make words Happen!

All fear
~ . is illusion,
but it can
also become
a reality.

cubicle key

10-21-08

drinking rum from a flask
while staring at algebra hw,
very sad...

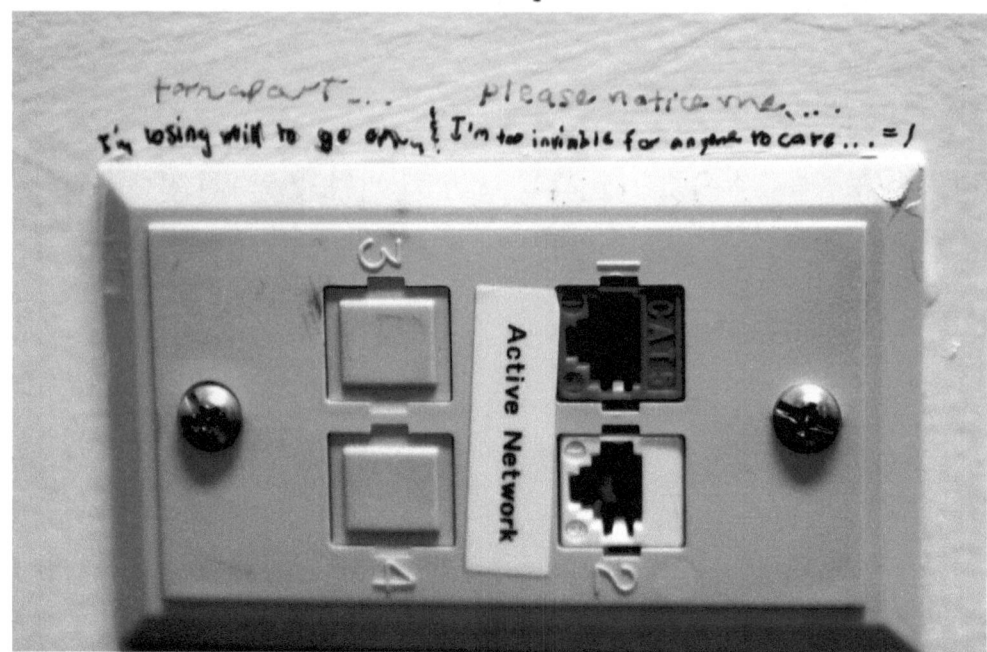

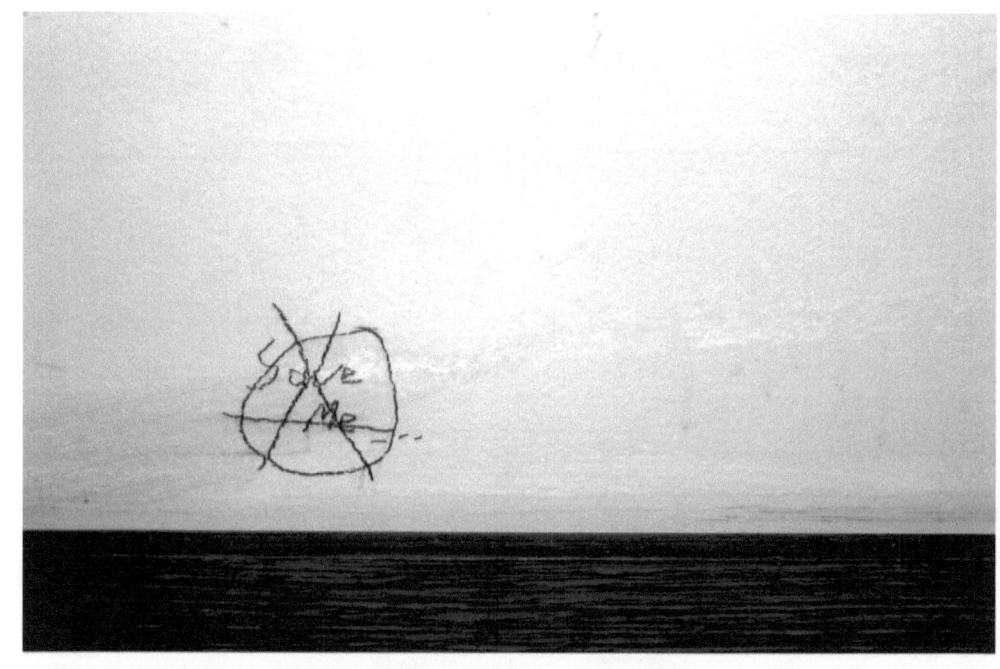

School Spirit

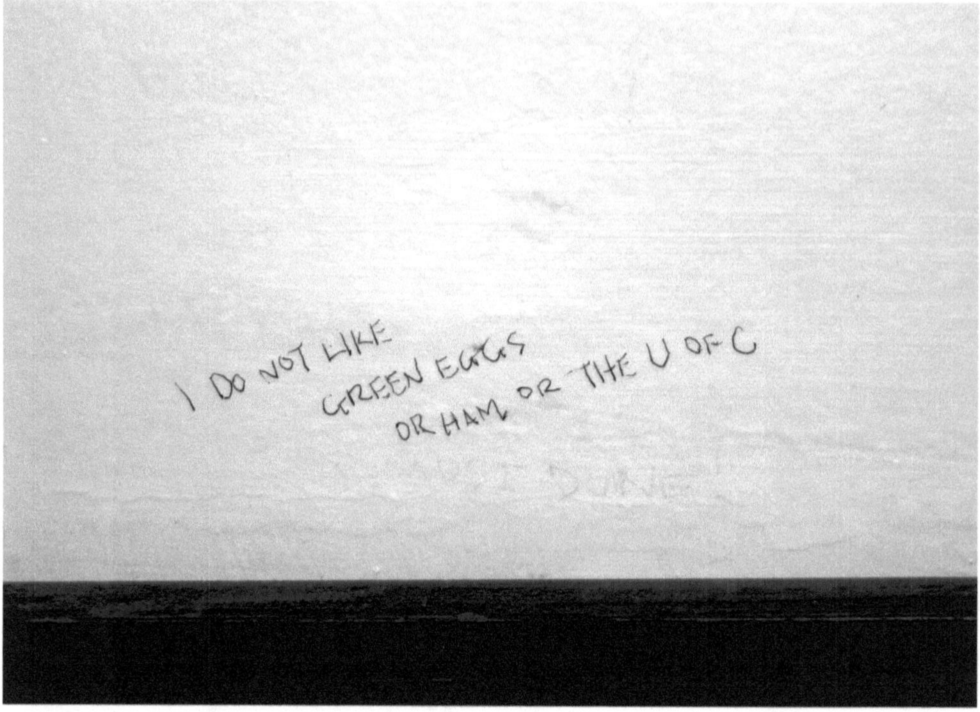

I DO NOT LIKE GREEN EGGS OR HAM OR THE U OF C

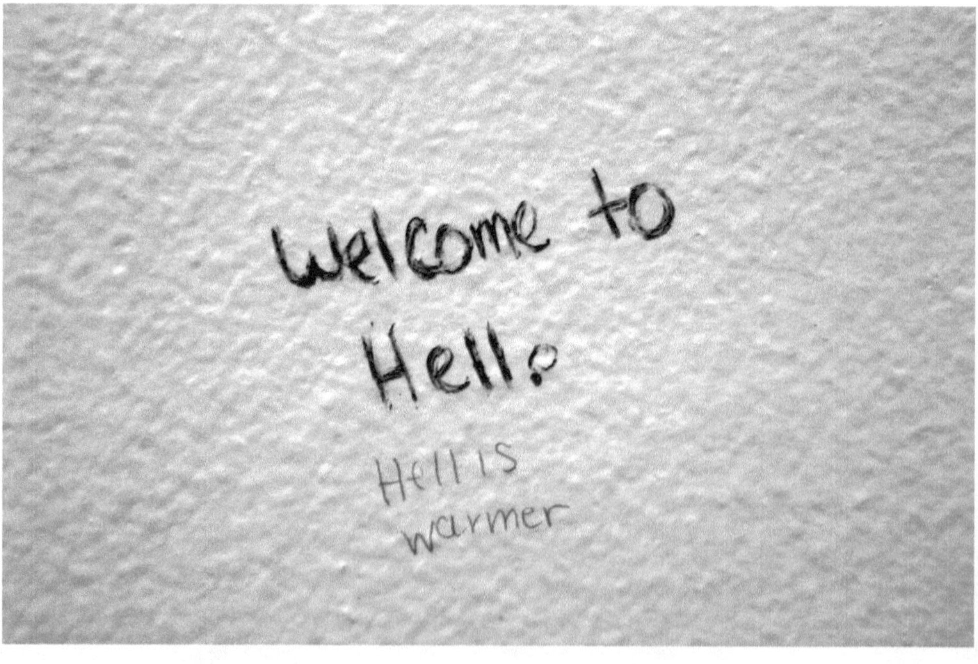

Welcome to Hell.

Hell is warmer

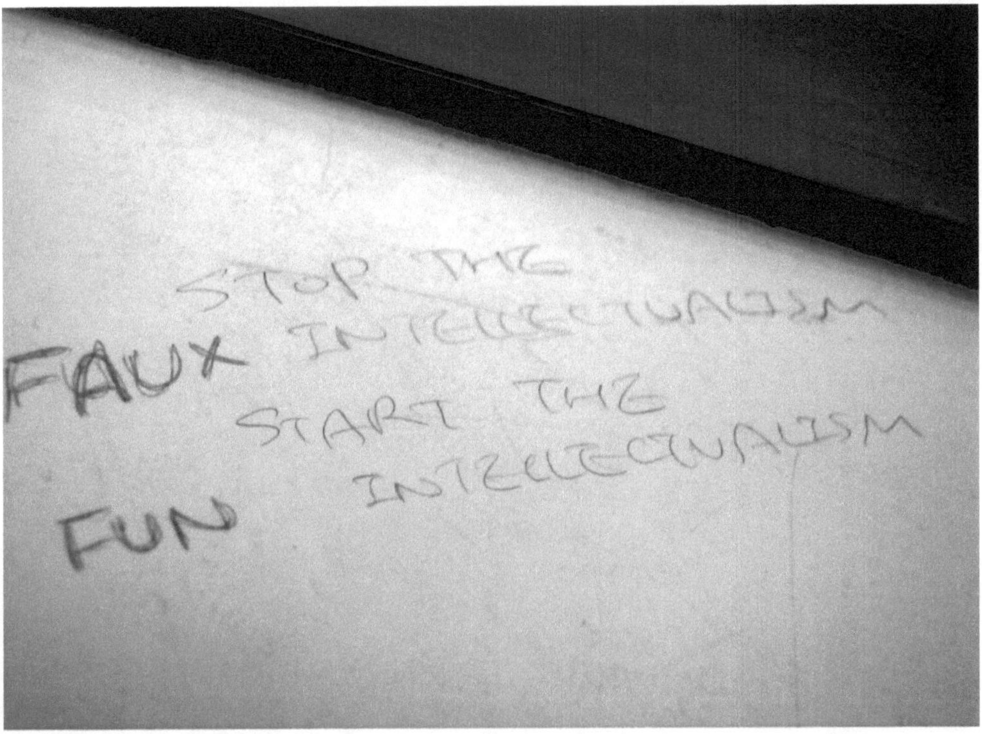

STOP THE
FAUX INTELLECTUALISM
START THE
FUN INTELLECTUALISM

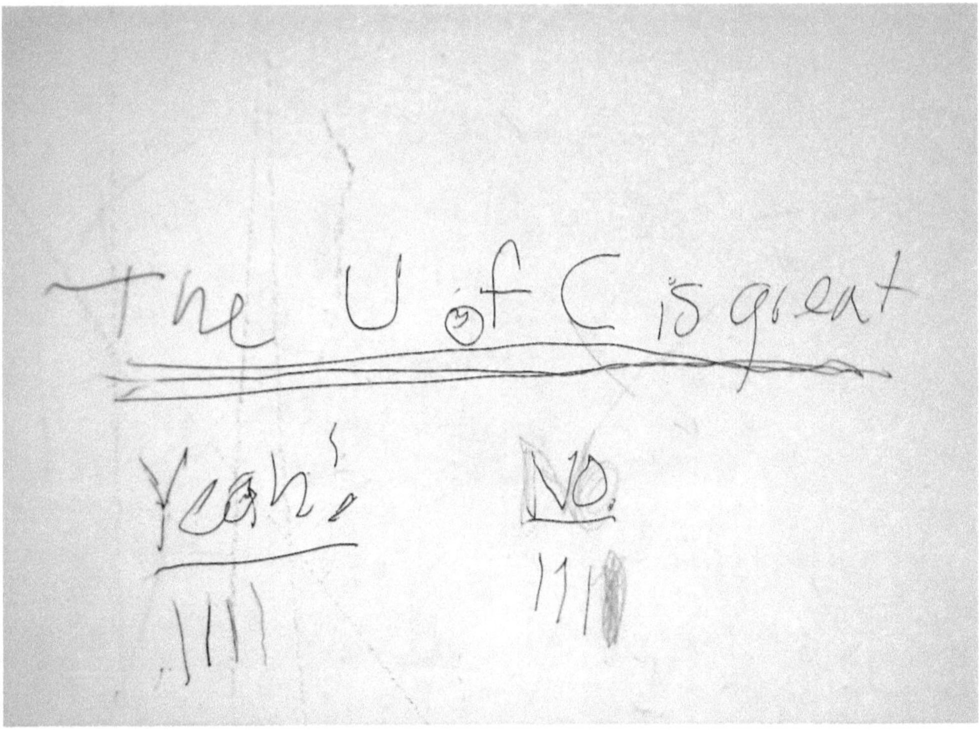

The U of C is great

Yeah!   NO.
||||| ||||

U Chicago
does not
know
how to
make its kids
smile.
      Evil mind has ⎯ B.S.
penetrated the
Soul of UChicago
and our tears
are inevitable.
for at least
4 years.
           ↳TRUE THA

Multilingual

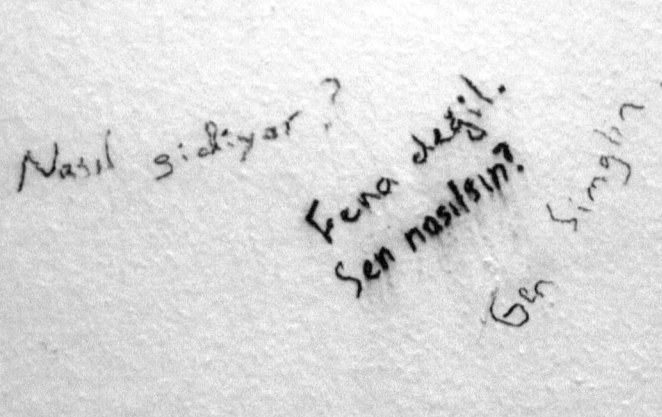

(Turkish) -How're you doing? -Not bad. And you? -[jibberish]

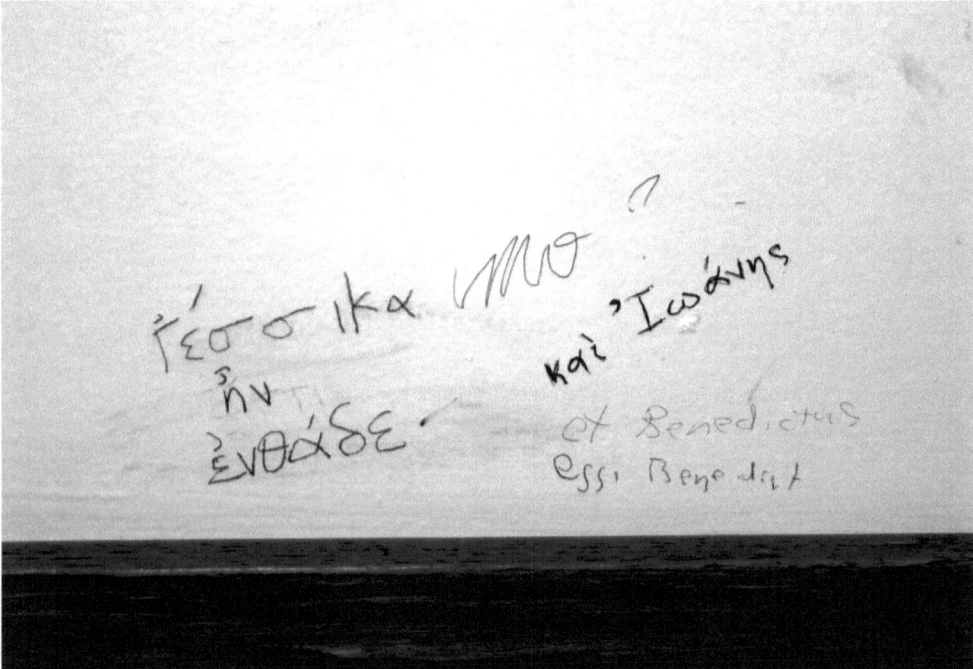

(Greek) -Jessica was here. [misspelled] -And John.
(Incorrect Latin) -Out of praise (English) -Eggs benedict

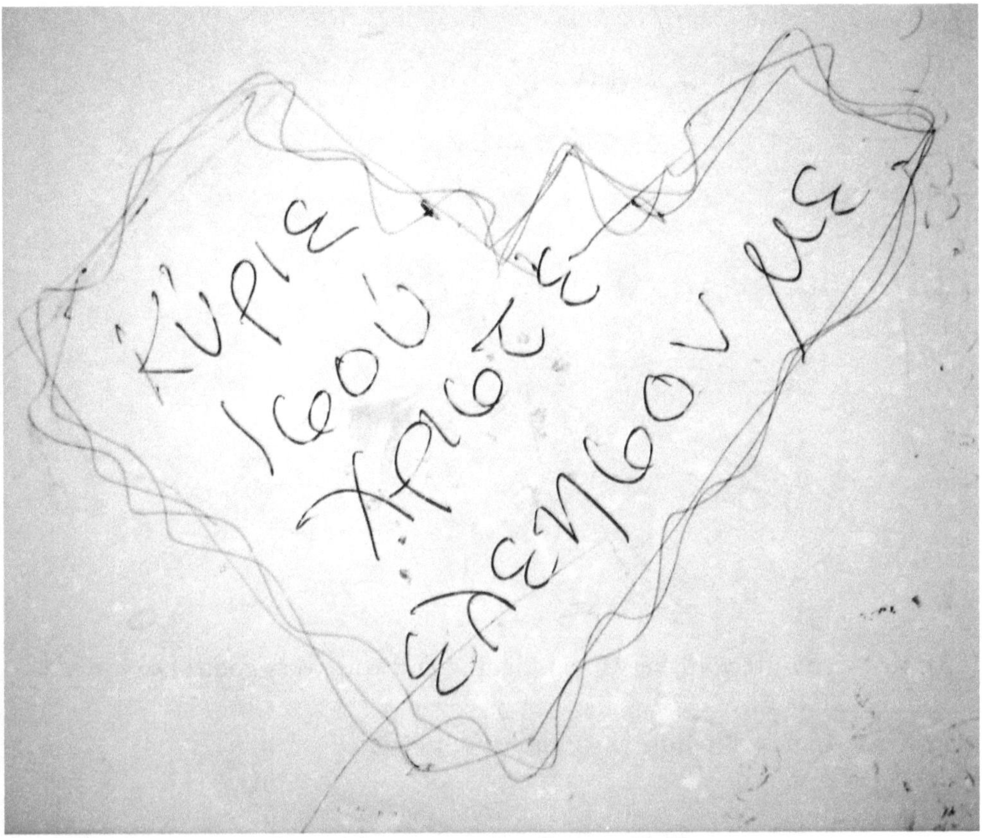

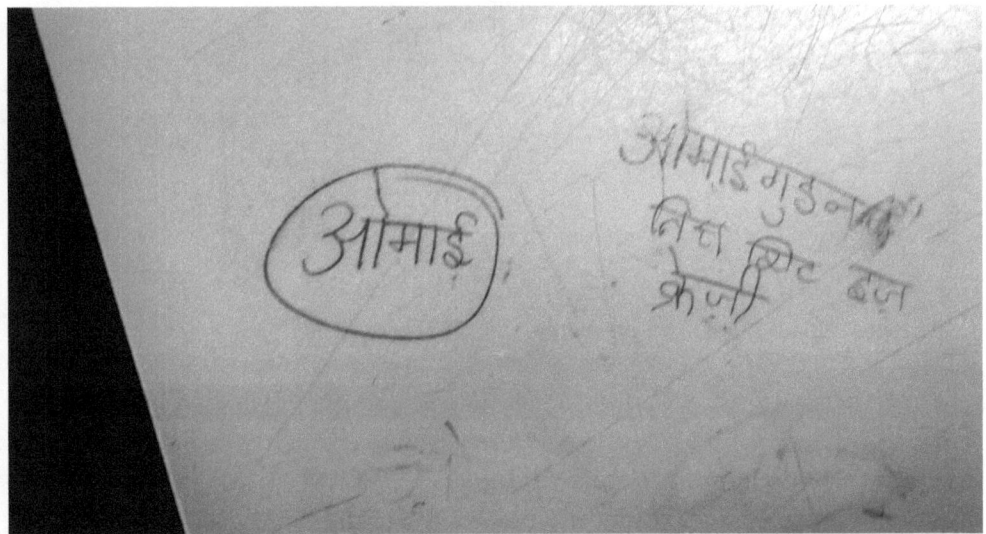

(Greek) -Lord Jesus Christ take pity on me. [misspelled]

(English written in Devanagari) -Oh my -Oh my goodness this shit is crazy

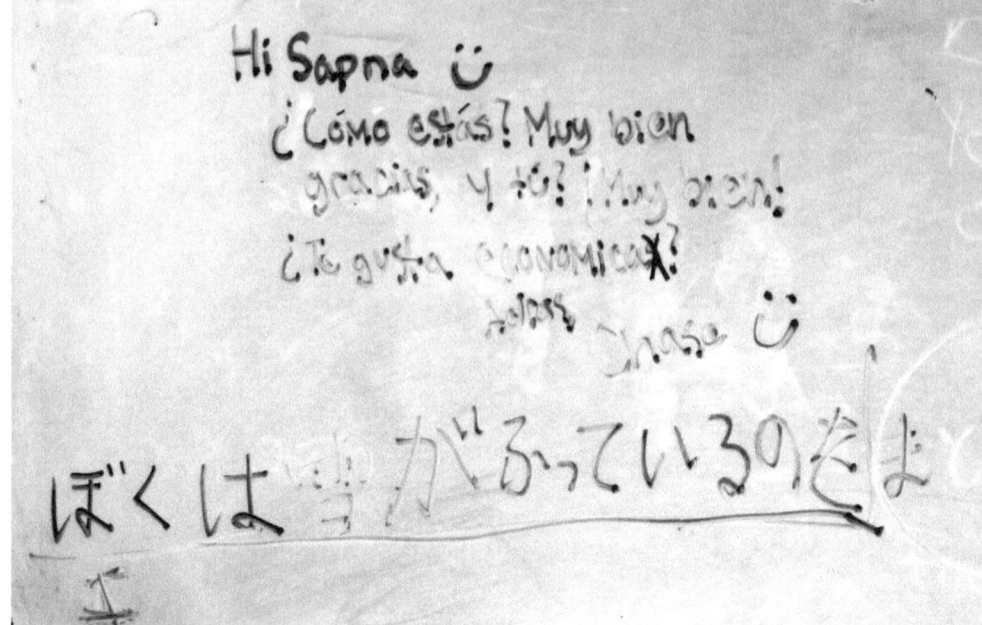

(Spanish) -How are you? Very good, thanks, and you? Very good! Do you like economics? Goodbye.

(Japanese) -I, snow is falling [incomplete sentence]

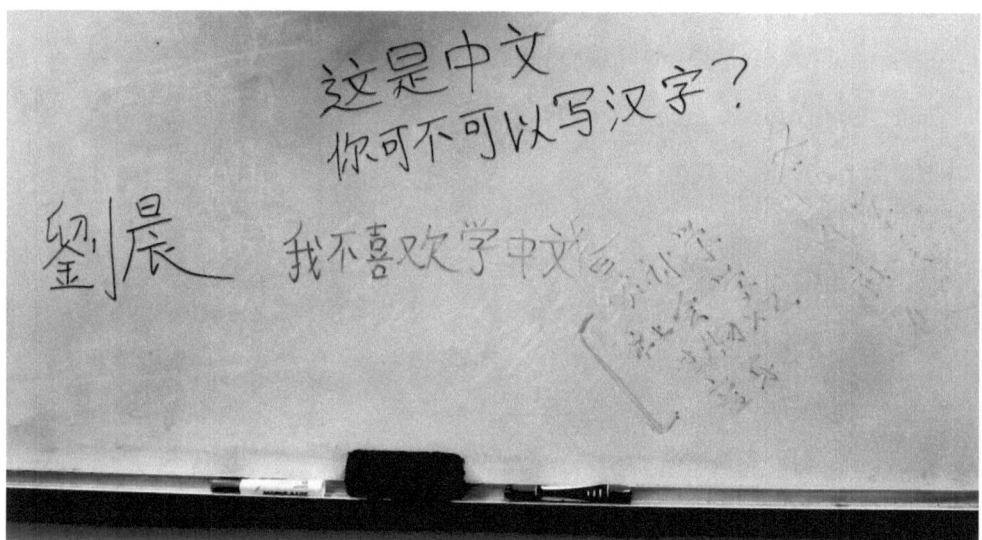

(Chinese) -This is Chinese. Can you write Chinese characters or not?
-Liu Chen   -I do not like to study Chinese
-Spring / Statistics / Sociology / Biology x 2 / Music
-Winter / Biology / Chemistry / Sociology / History

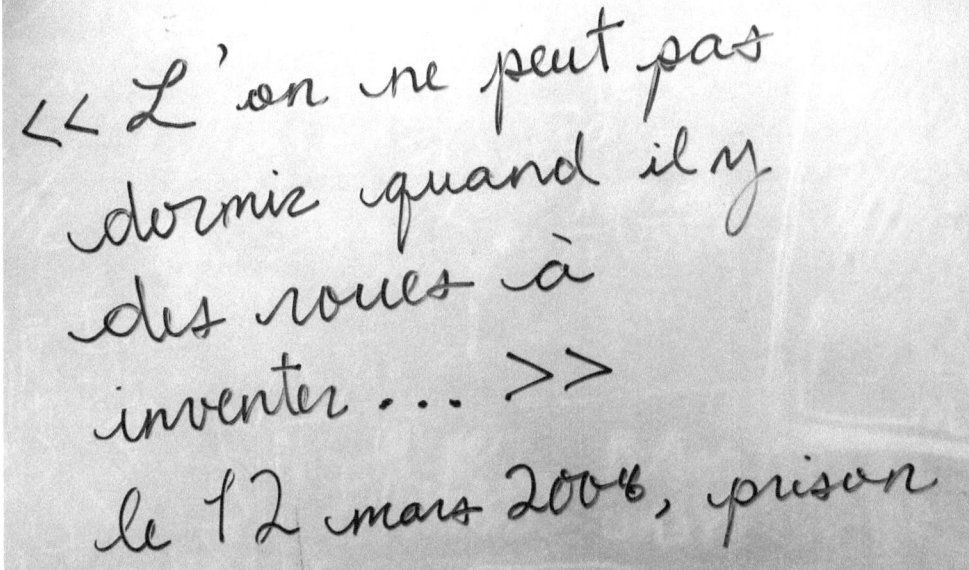

(French) -One cannot sleep while there are wheels to invent.
12 March 2008, prison

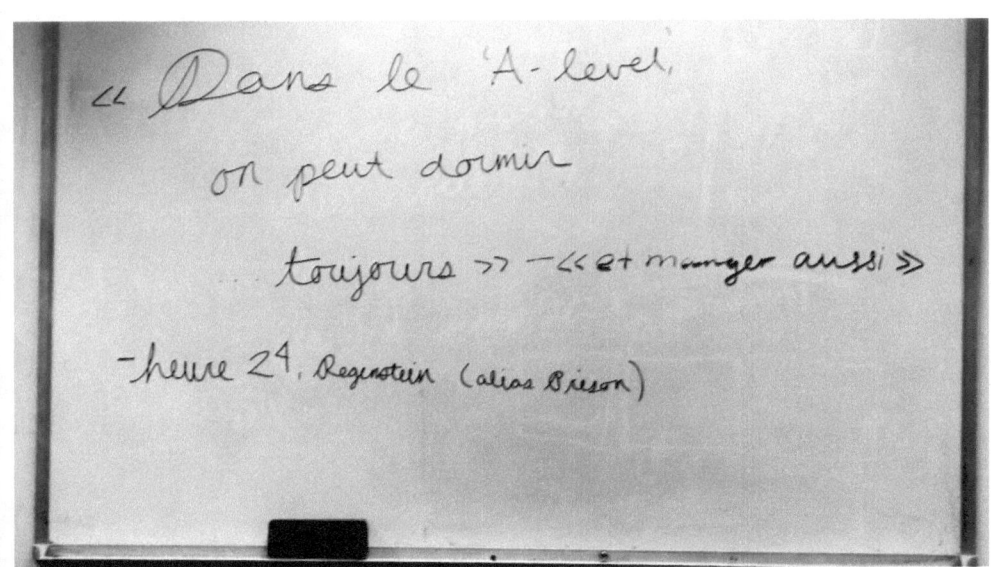

(French) -"On the 'A-level' a nap today" - "and eat too"
-hour 24, Regenstein (alias 'prison')

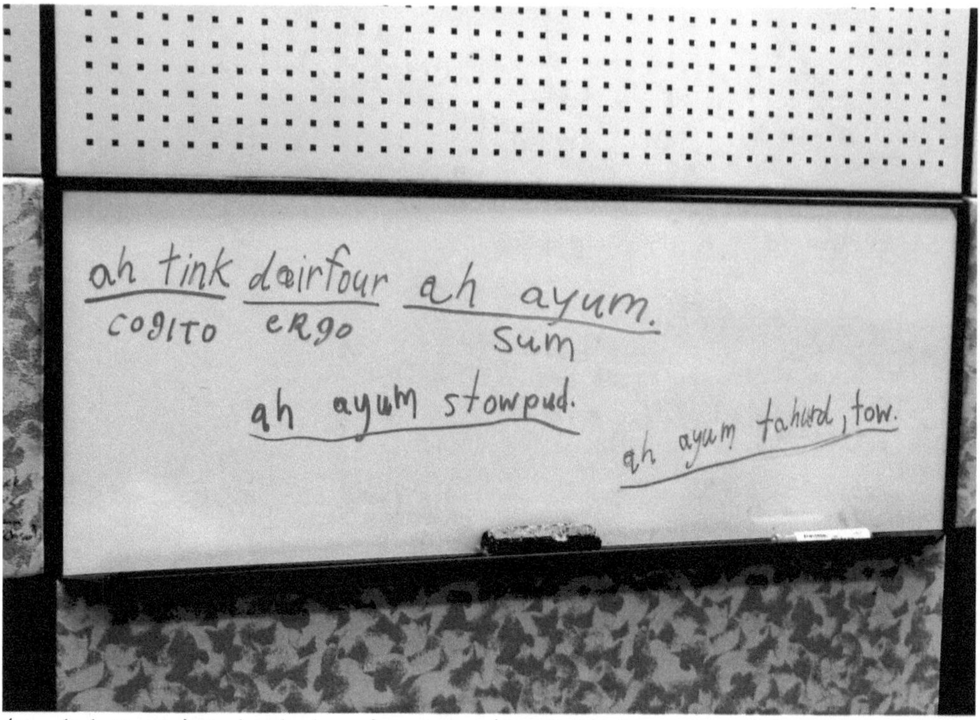

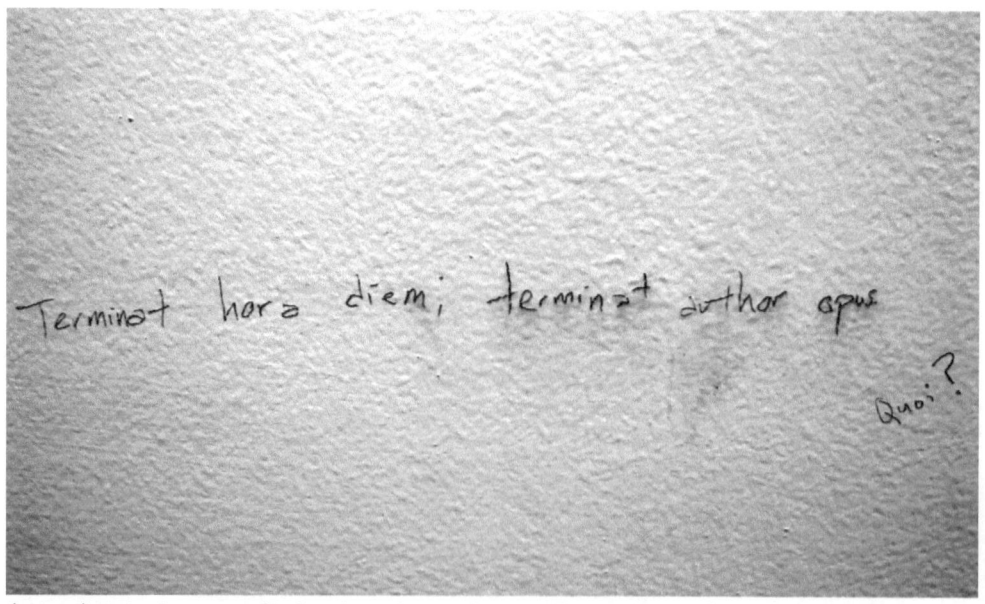

(English/Latin) -I think therefore I am. (English) -I am stupid. -I am tired too.

(Latin) -The hour ends the day, the author ends his work. (French) -What?

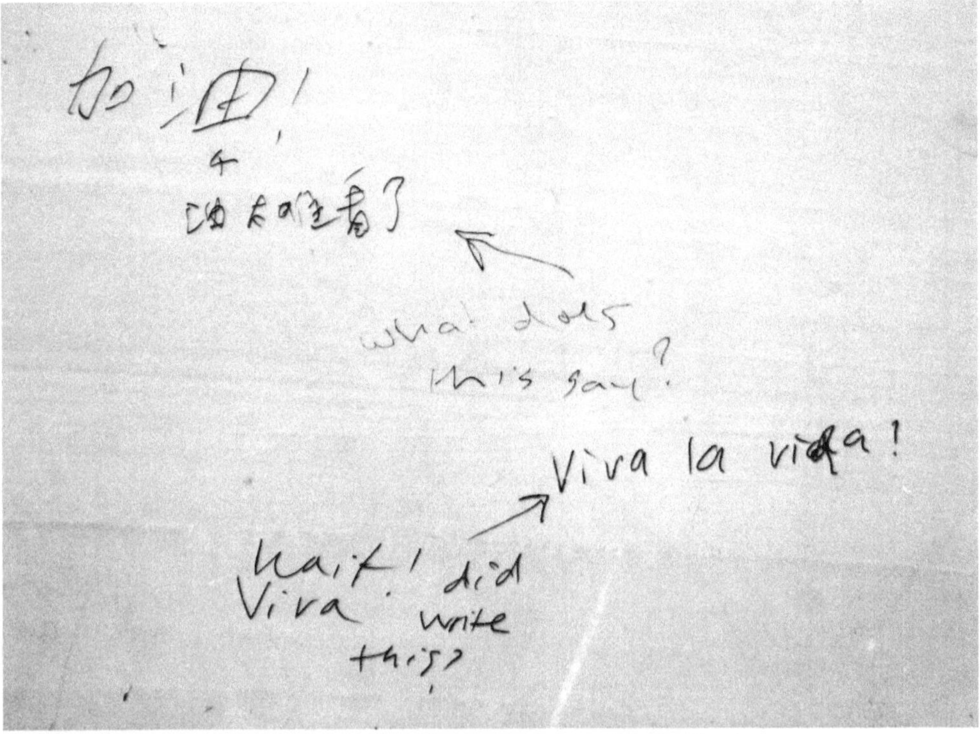

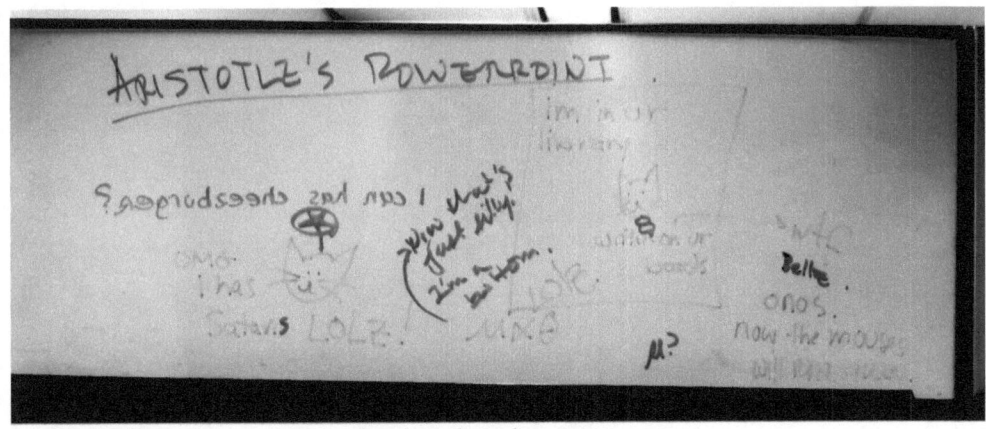

(Chinese) -Add gas! [a phrase for cheering on one's team]
-Gas too ugly-looking [probably saying the character is badly written]
(English) -What does this say?
(Spanish) -Long live life! [can also be used similarly to 'yay!']
(English) -Wait! Did Viva write this?

(LOLCat) See http://www.icanhascheezburger.com

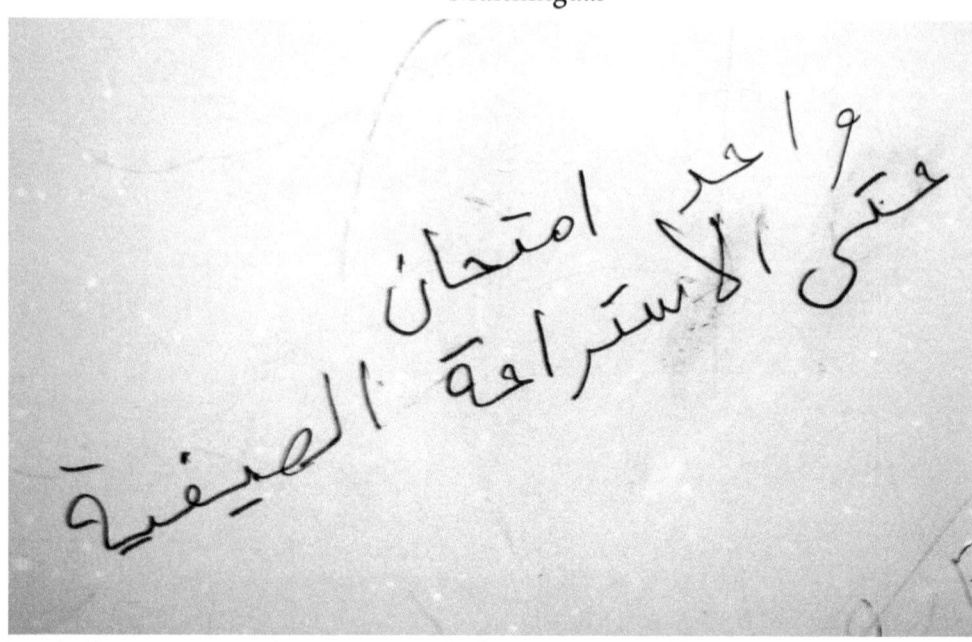

(Arabic) One test until summer break. [with a small grammar mistake]

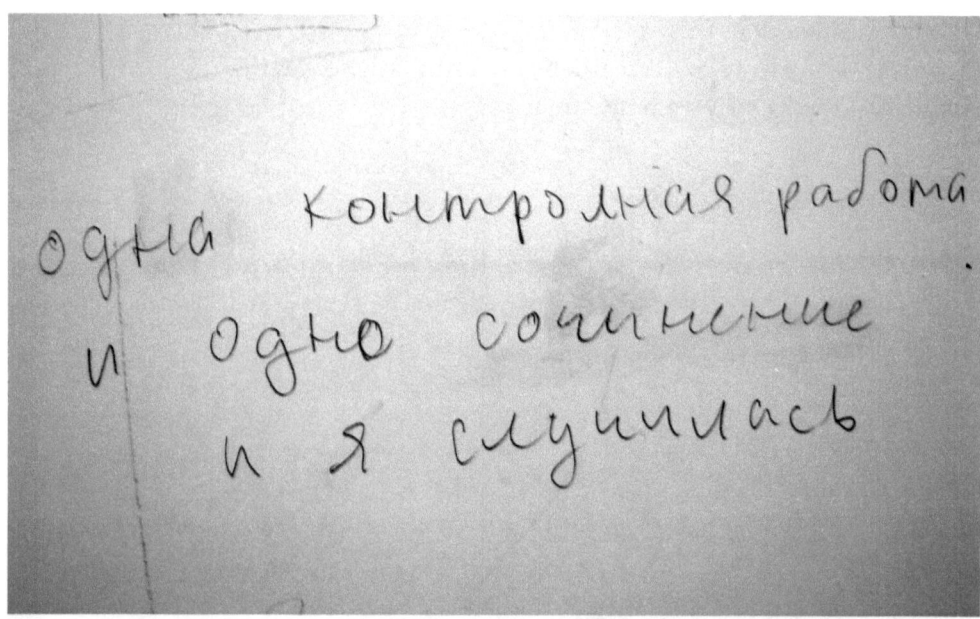

(Russian) One test and one essay and I happened. [probably meant to say "and I'm done"]

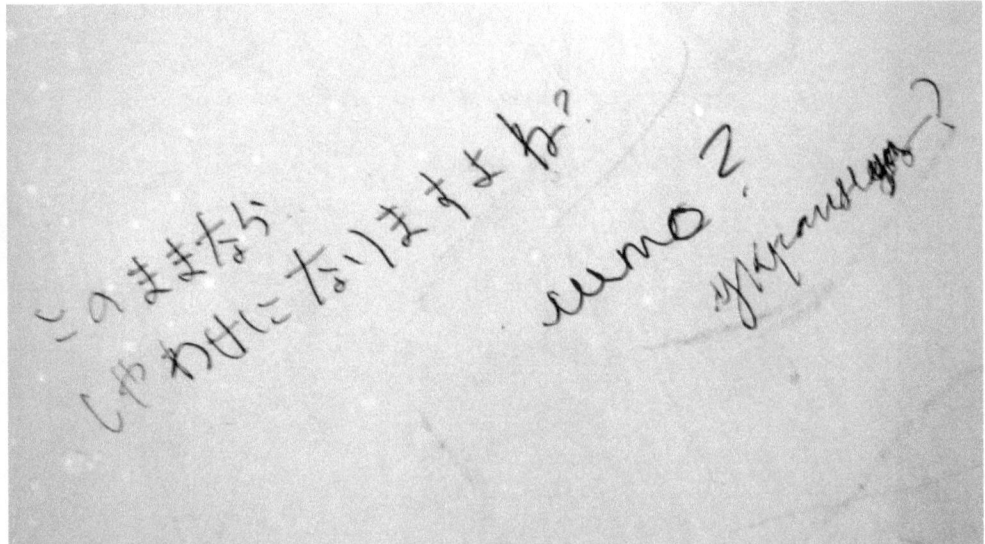

(Japanese) If things don't change, happiness is on the way, isn't it?
(Belarusian/Macedonian/Serbian/misspelled Russian) What?
(poorly written Russian) Ukrainians?

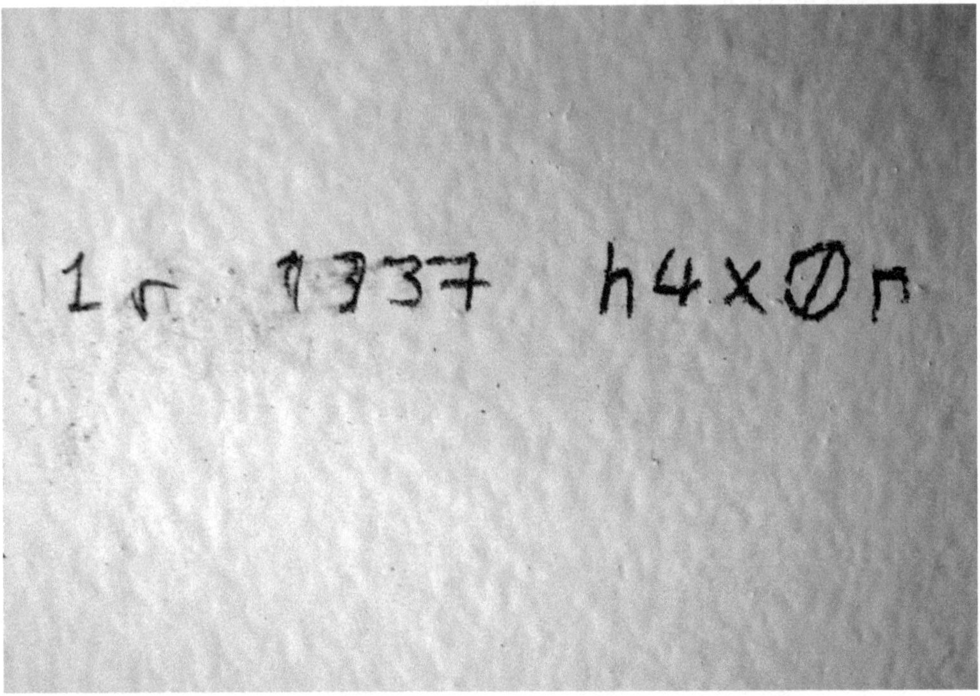

(Leetspeak) I am an elite hacker. [See http://en.wikipedia.org/wiki/Leet]

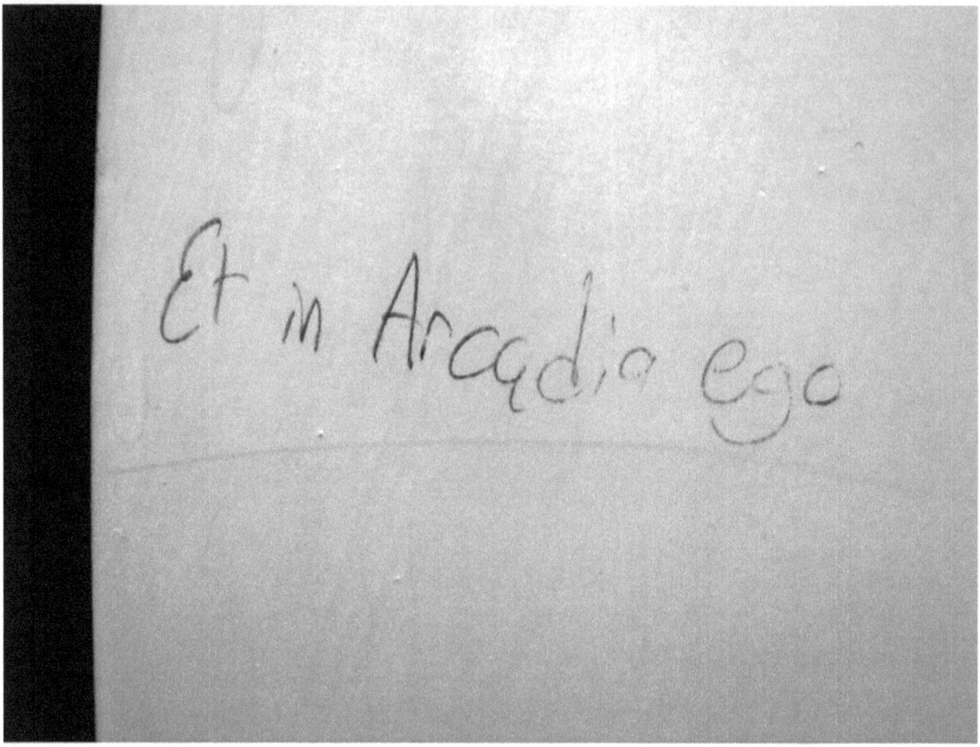

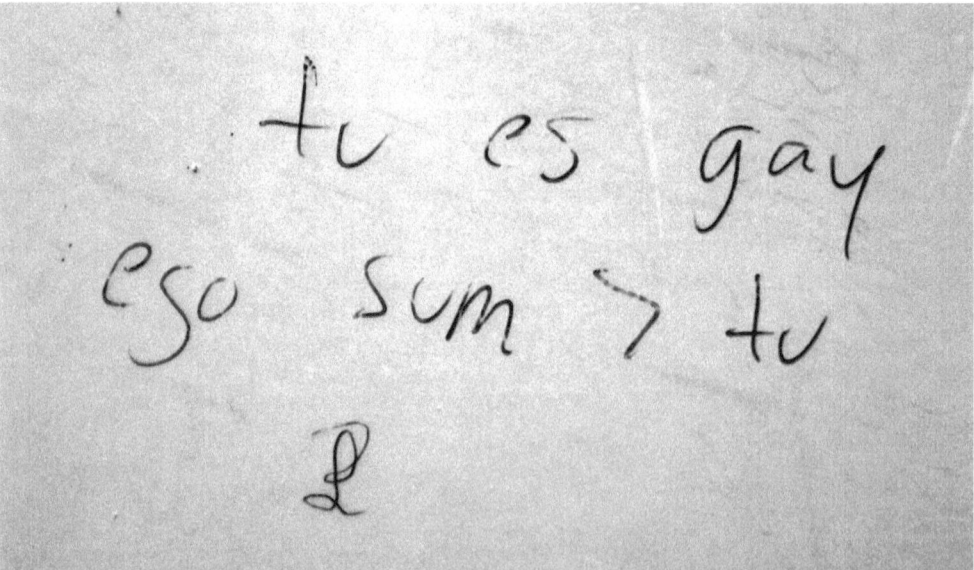

(Latin) Even in Arcadia I exist. [See http://en.wikipedia.org/wiki/
Et_in_Arcadia_ego]

(Latin) You are gay. I am better than you.

Doodles

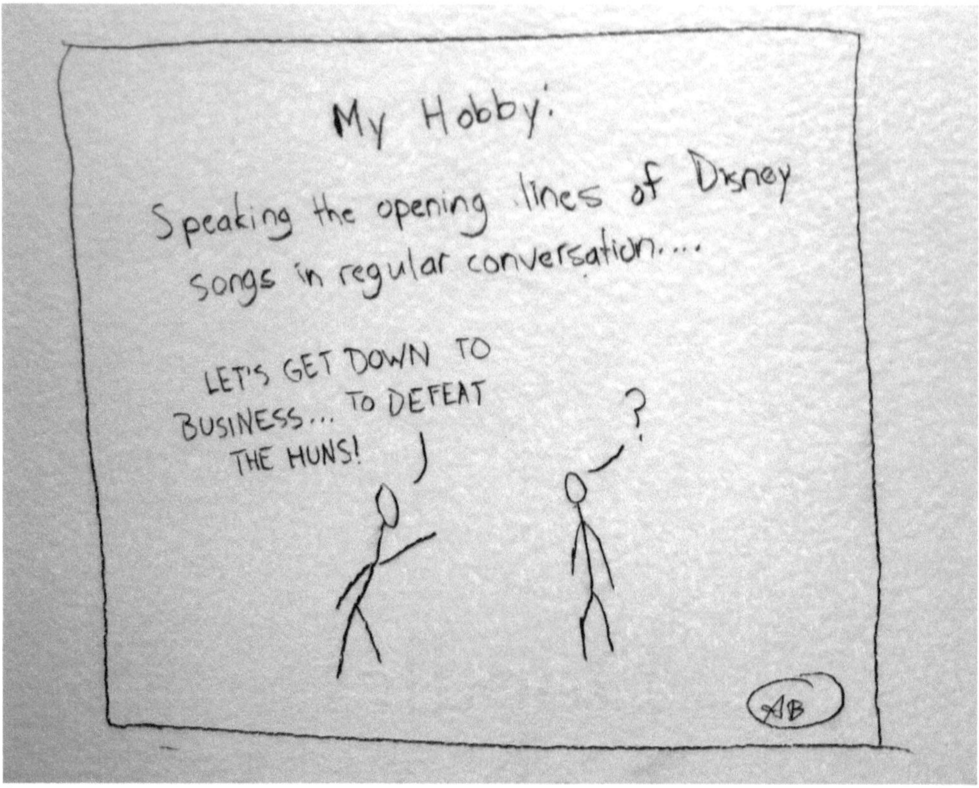

(See xkcd.com)

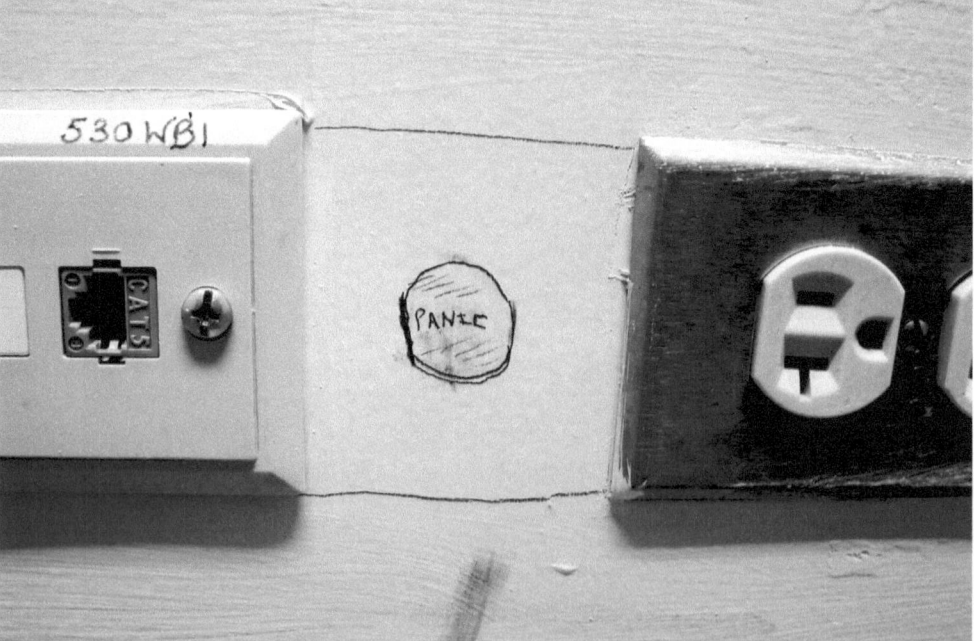

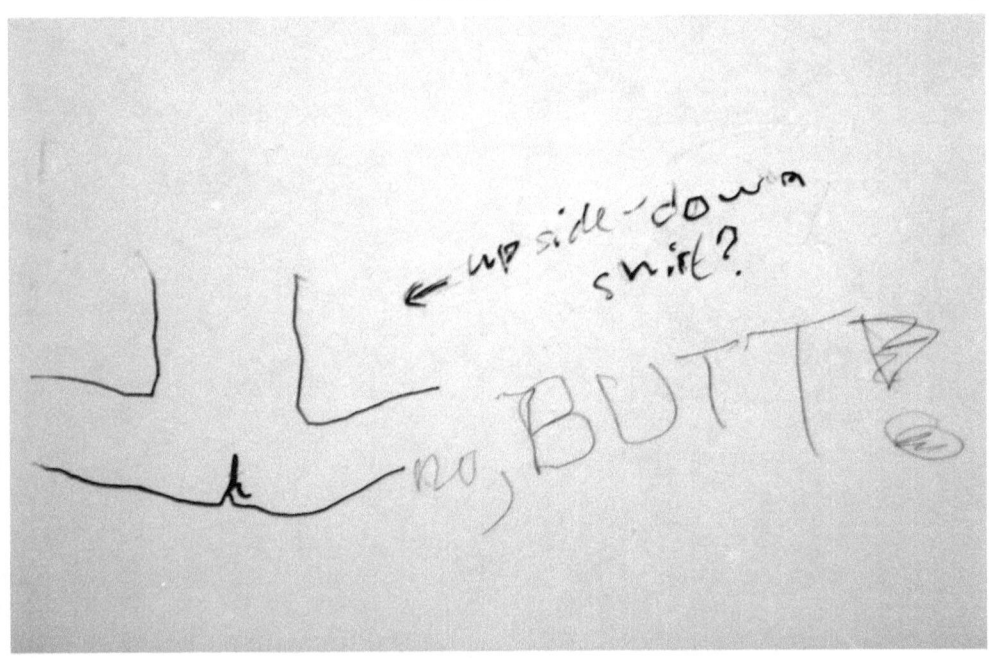

Doodles 65

upside-down shirt?

no, BUTT?

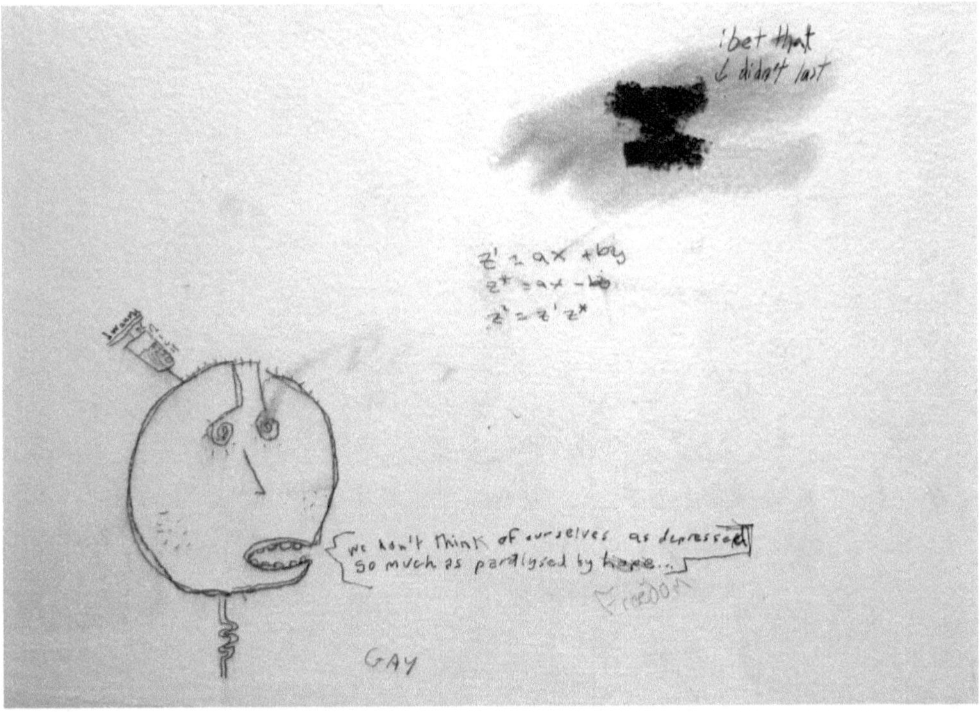

i bet that
it didn't last

$z' = ax + by$
$z^* = ax - by$
$z' = z' z^*$

we don't think of ourselves as depressed
so much as paralysed by hope...

freedom

GAY

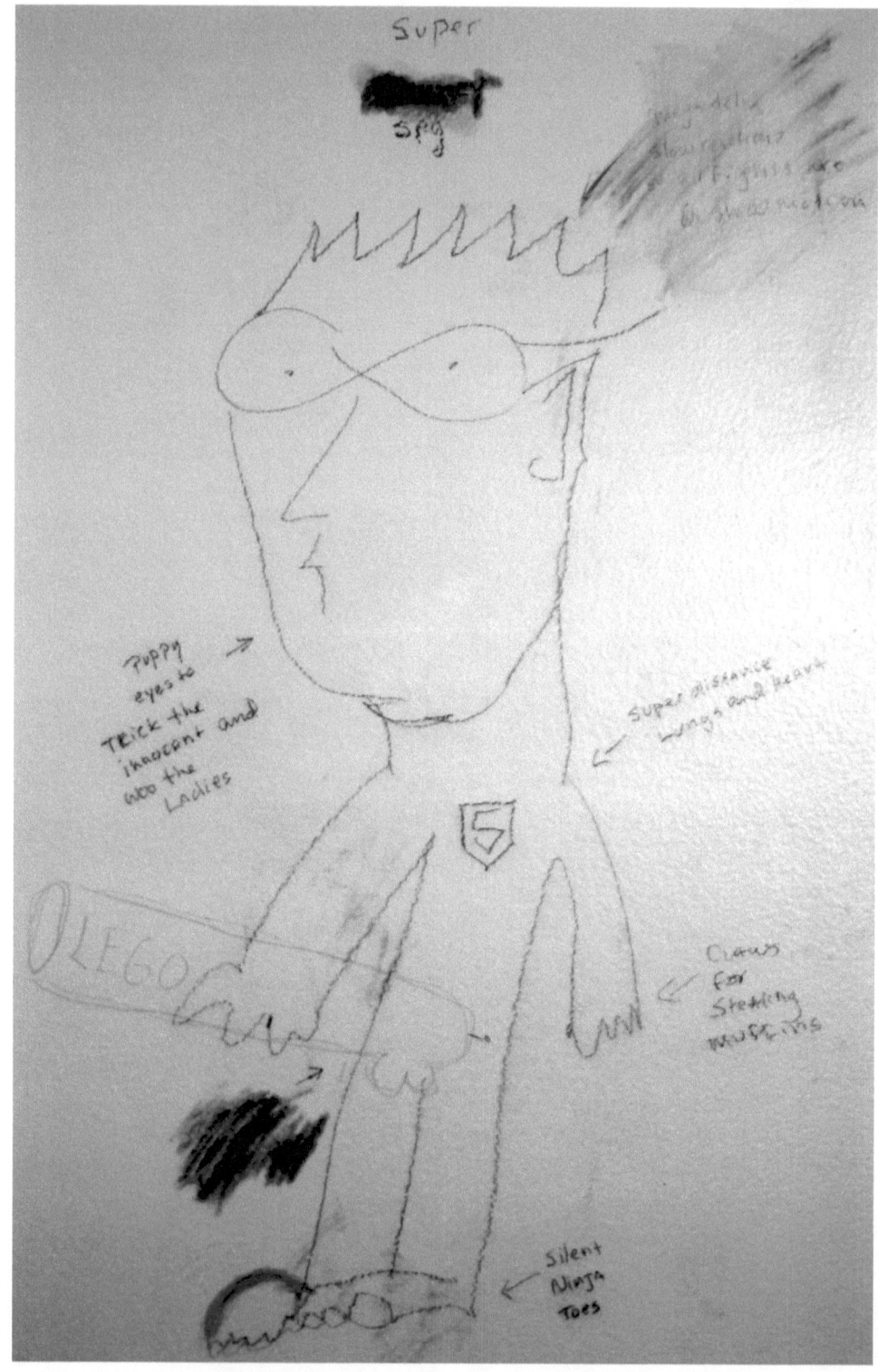

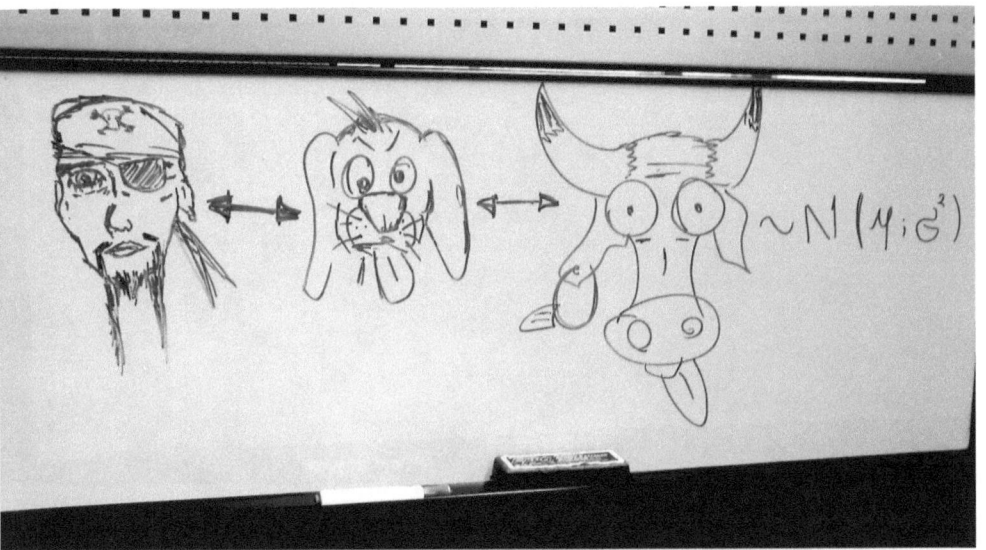

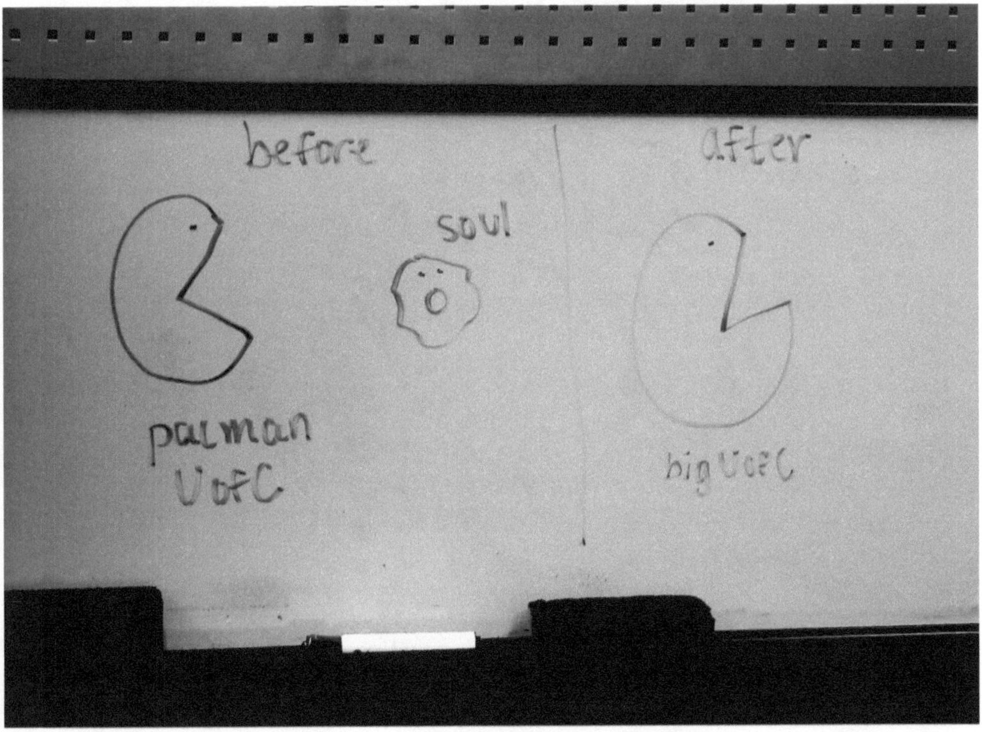

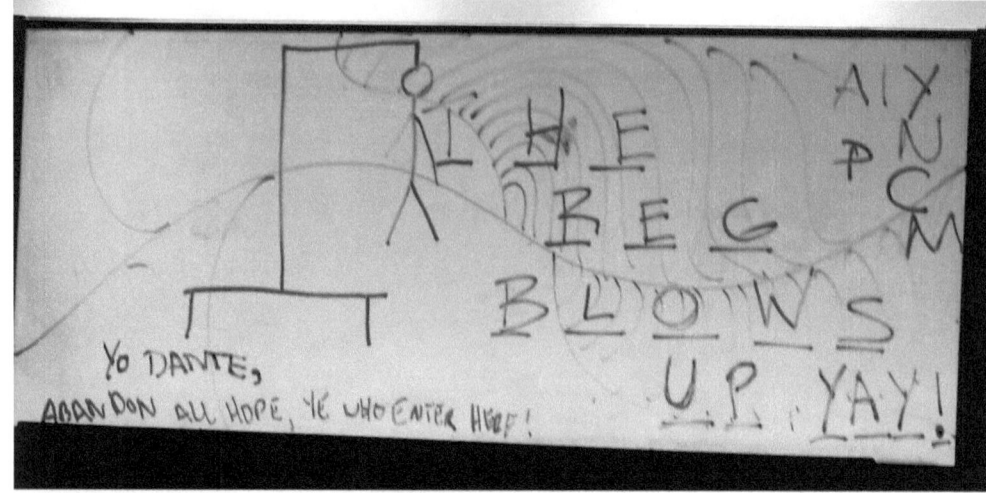

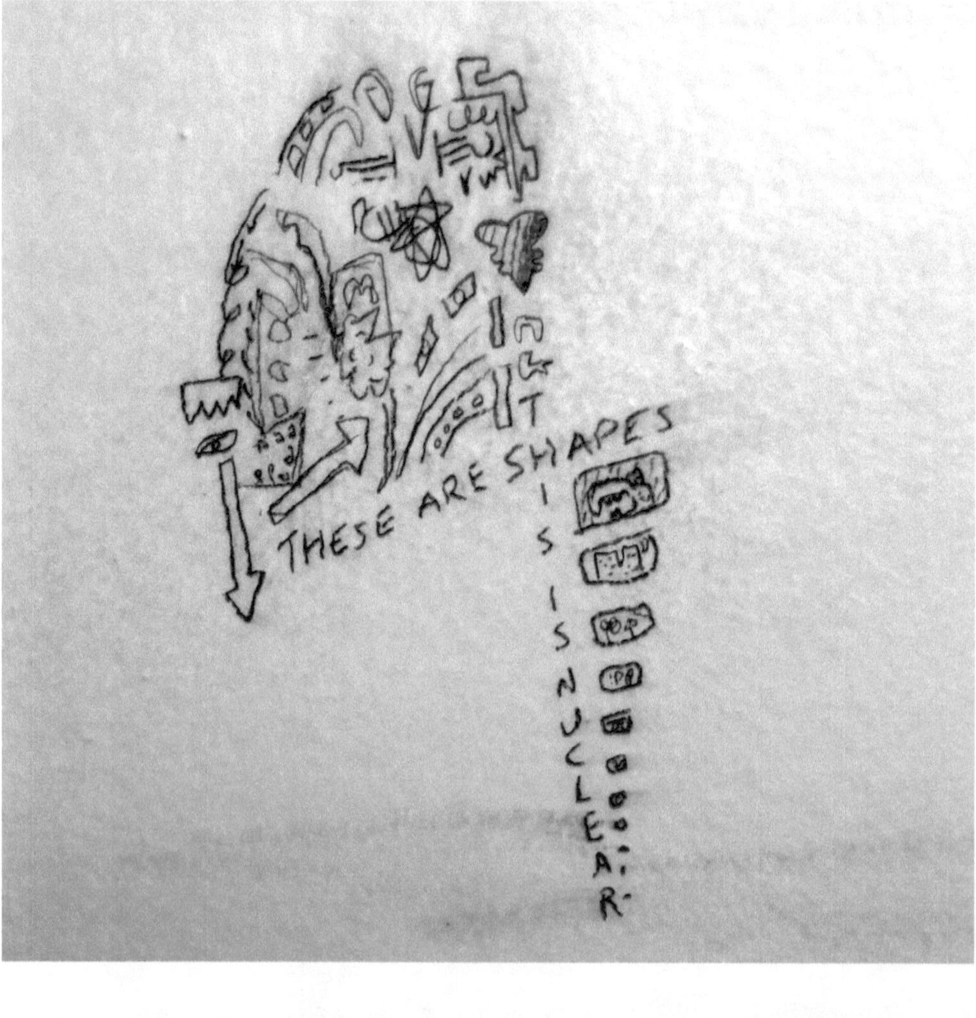

THESE ARE SHAPES

THIS IS NUCLEAR.

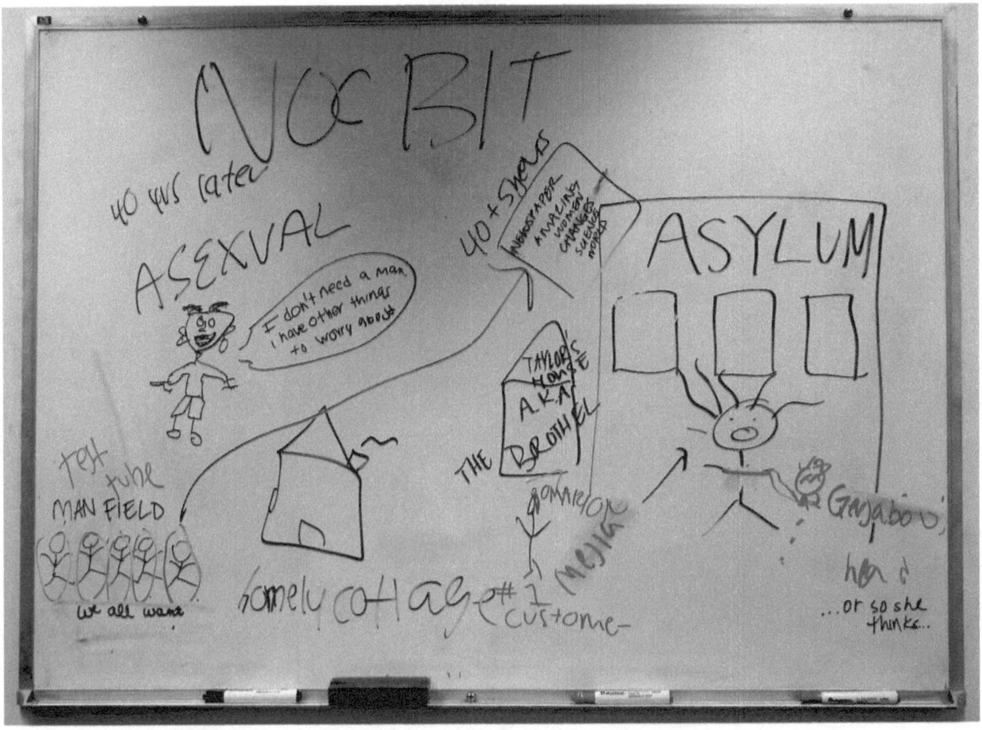

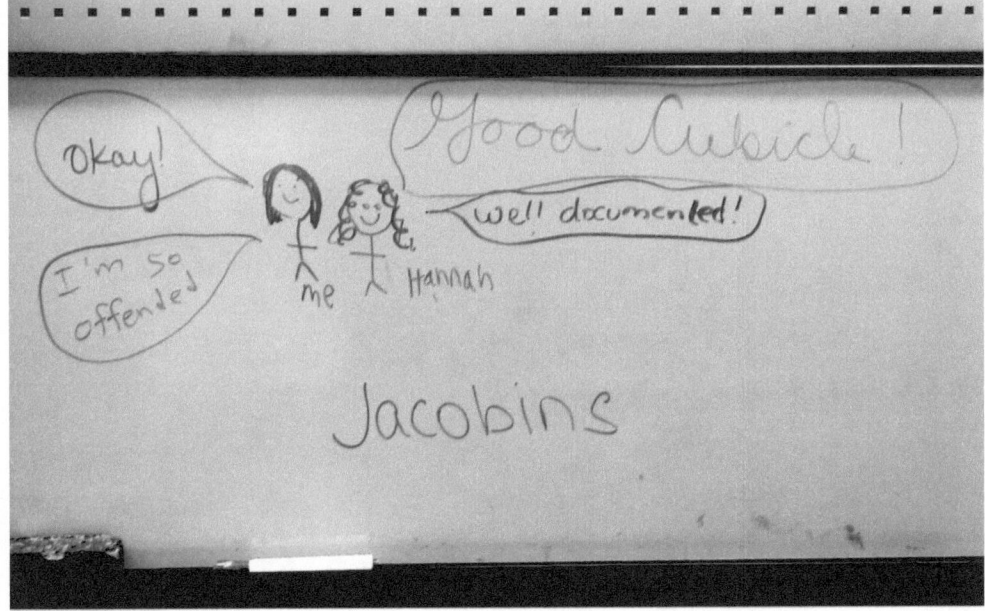

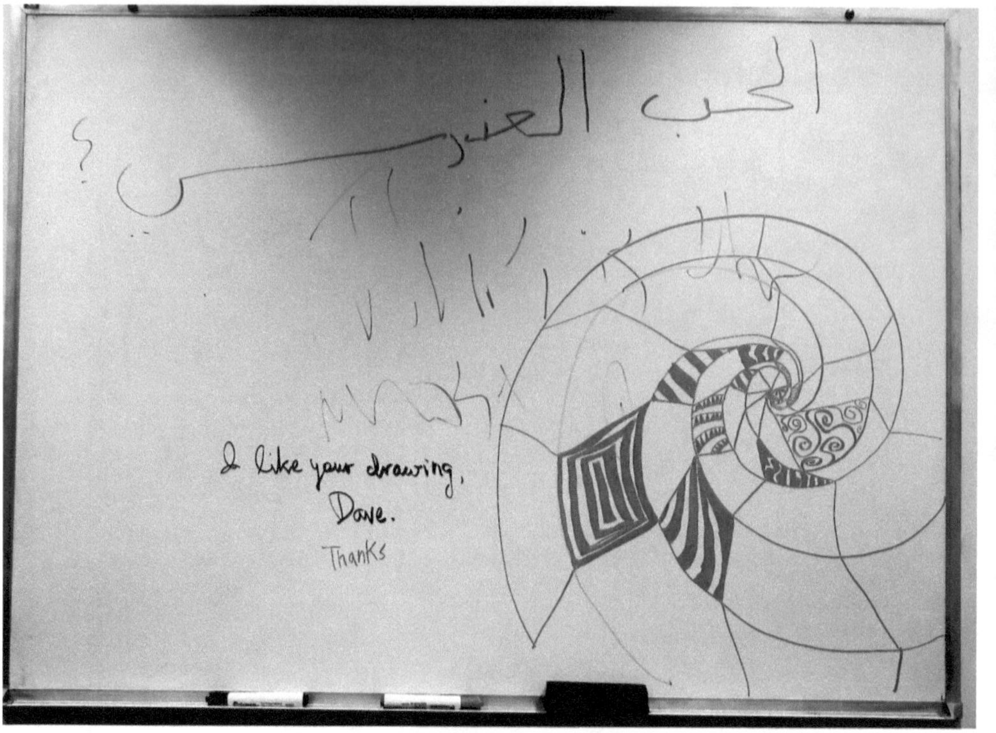

الحب العذري ؟

I like your drawing,
Dave.
Thanks

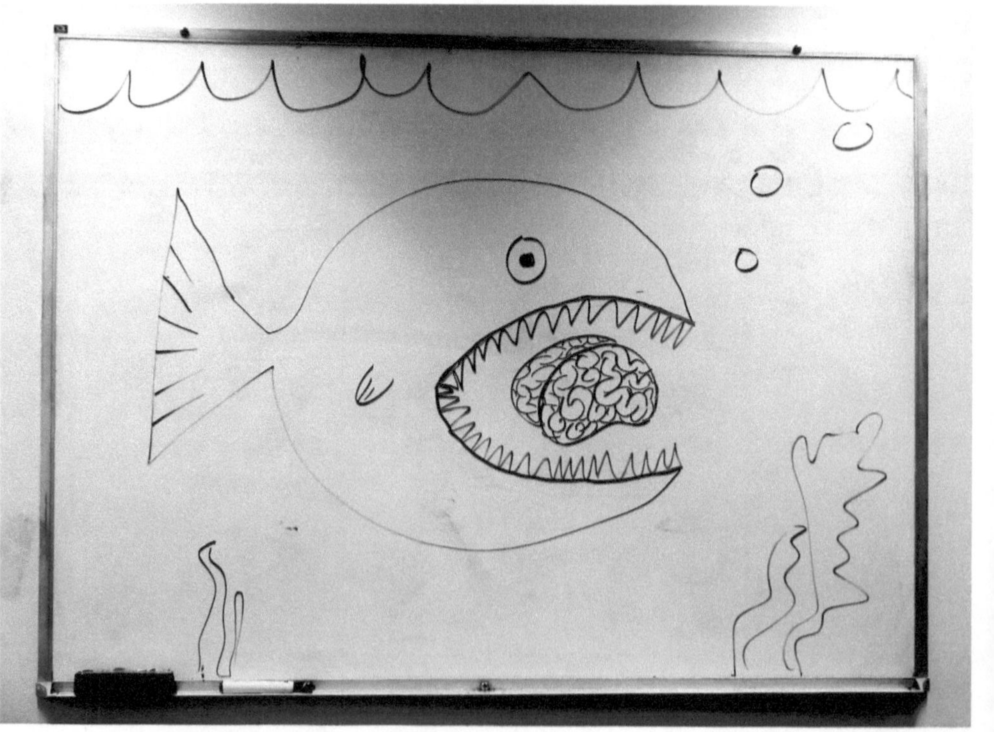

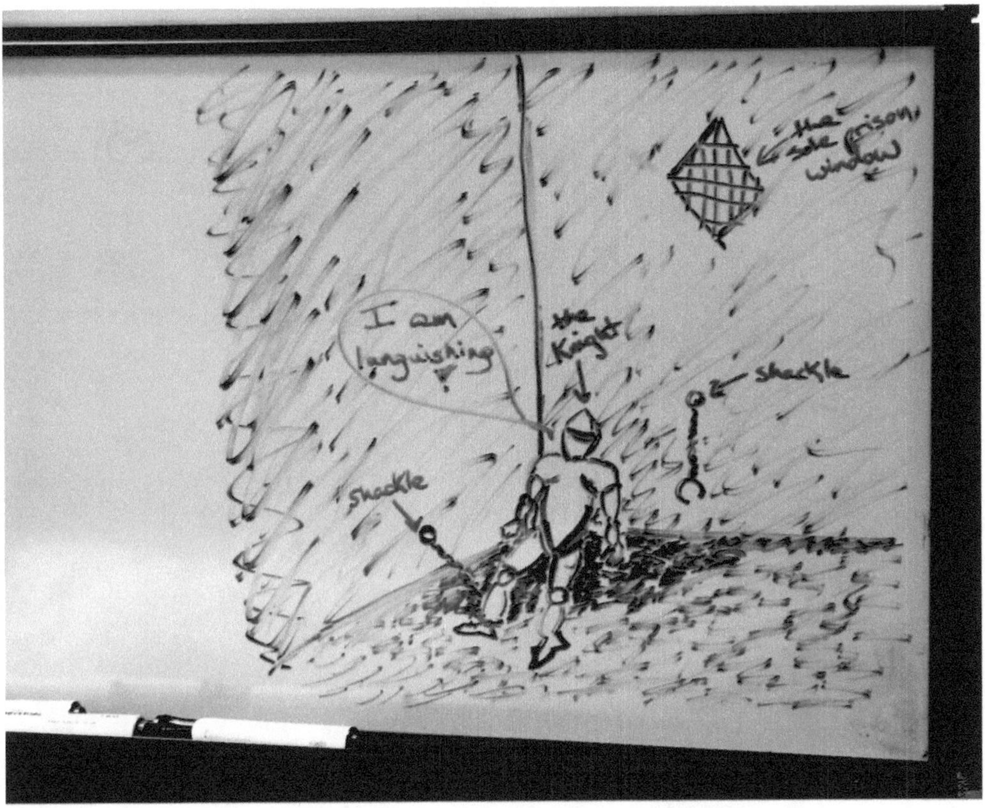

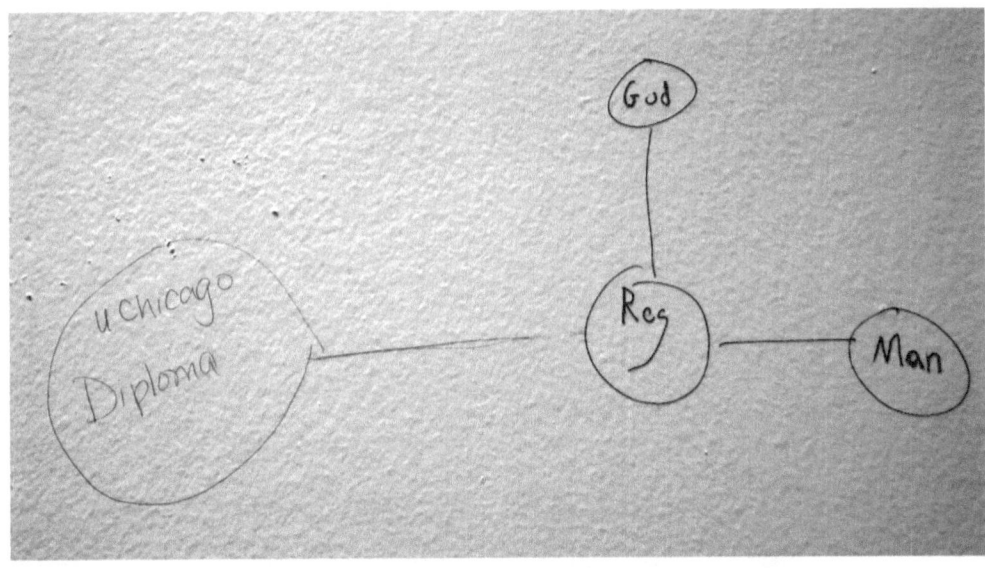

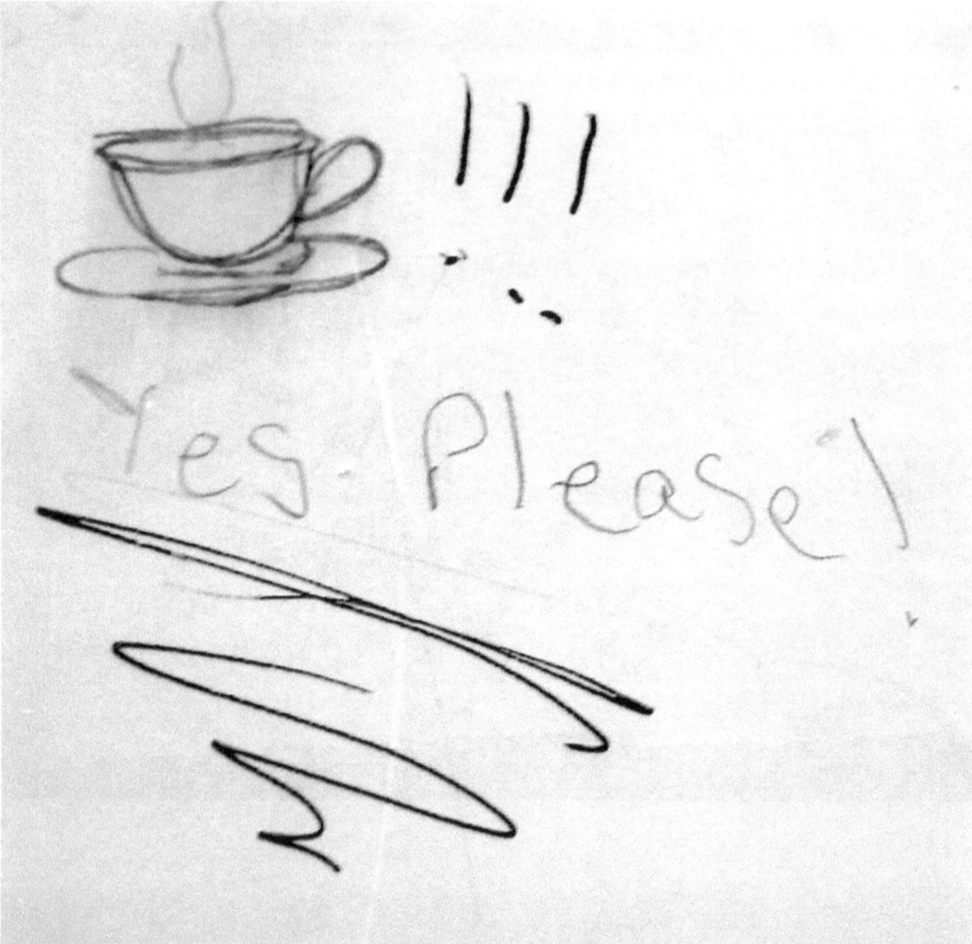

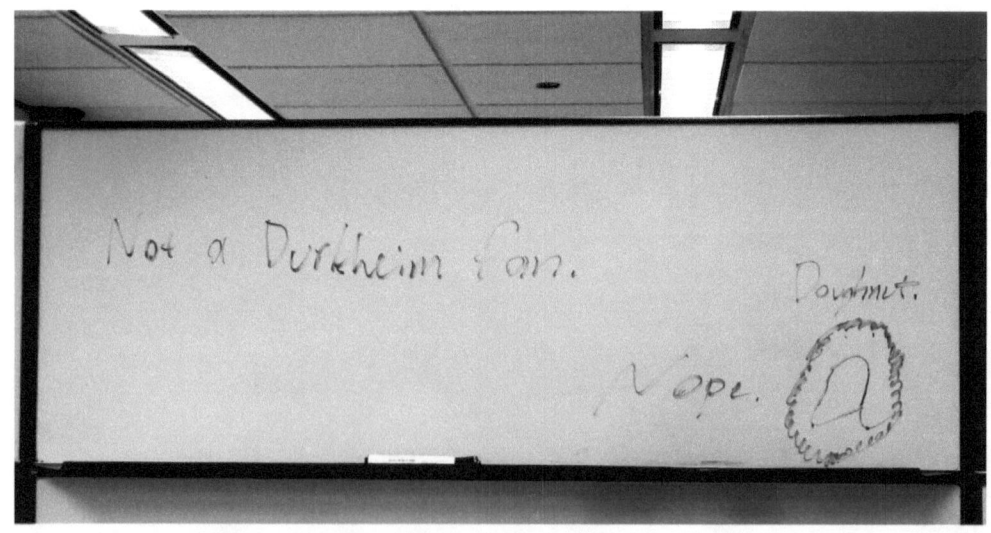

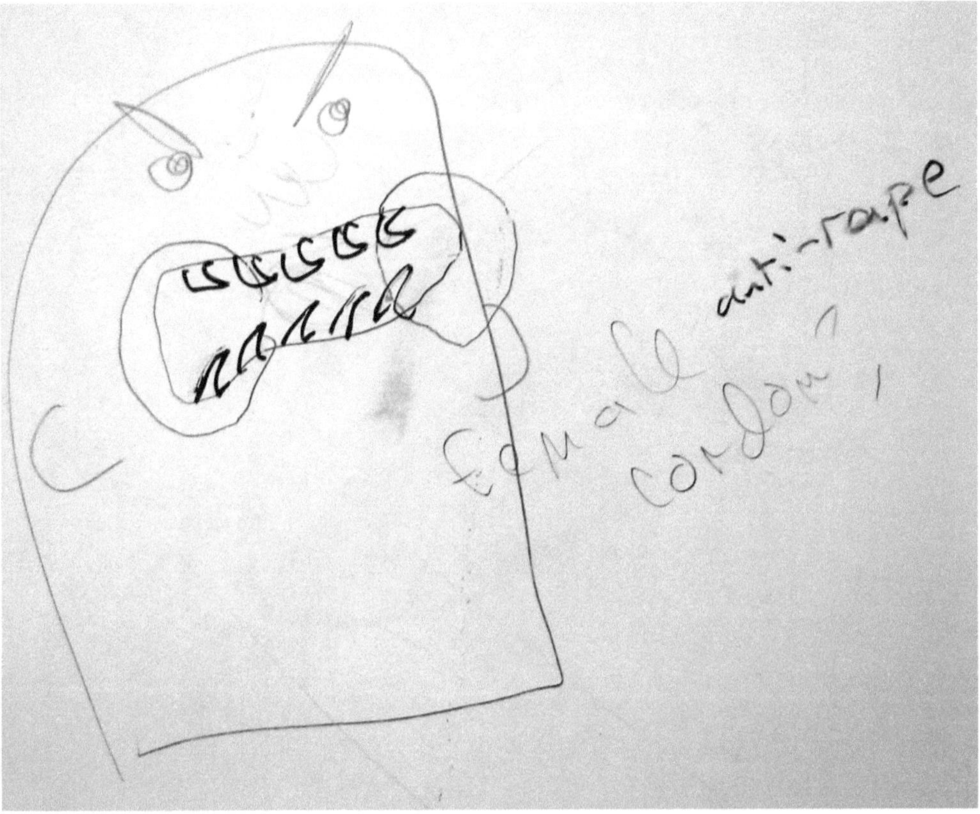

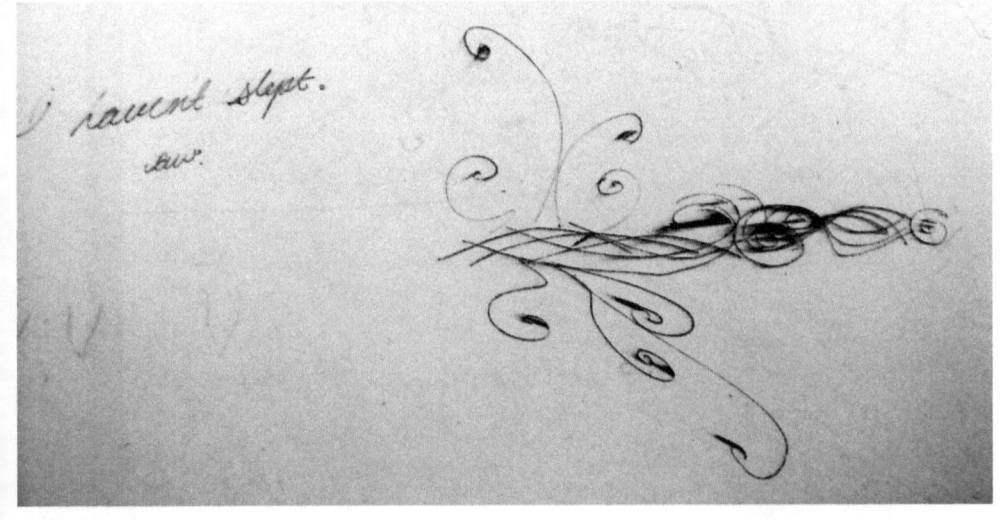

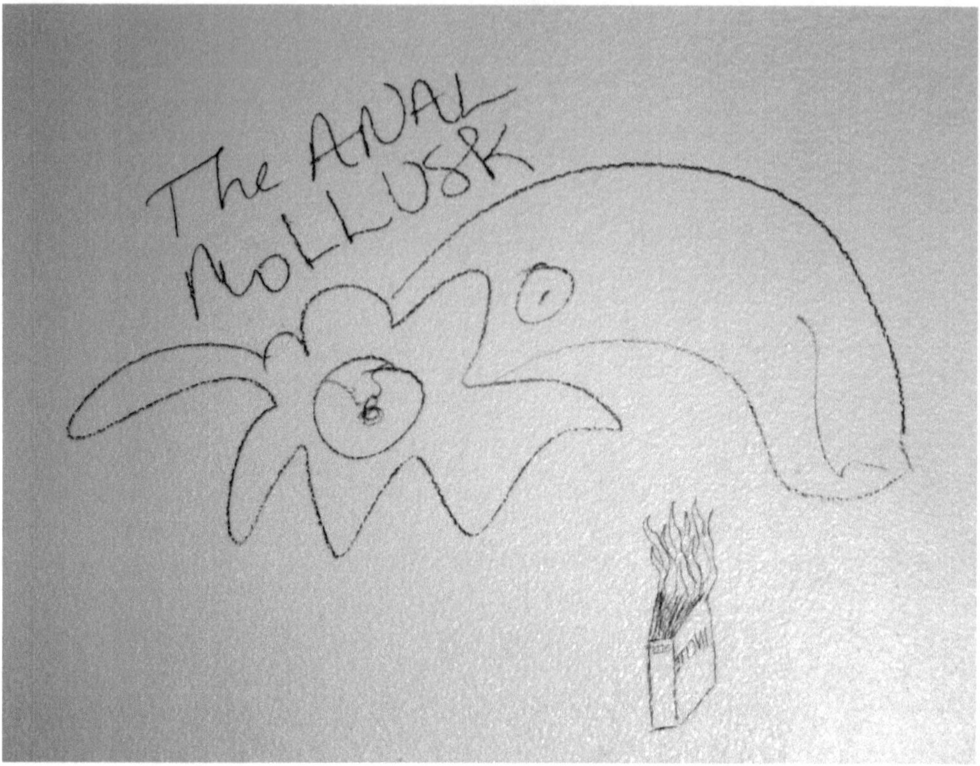

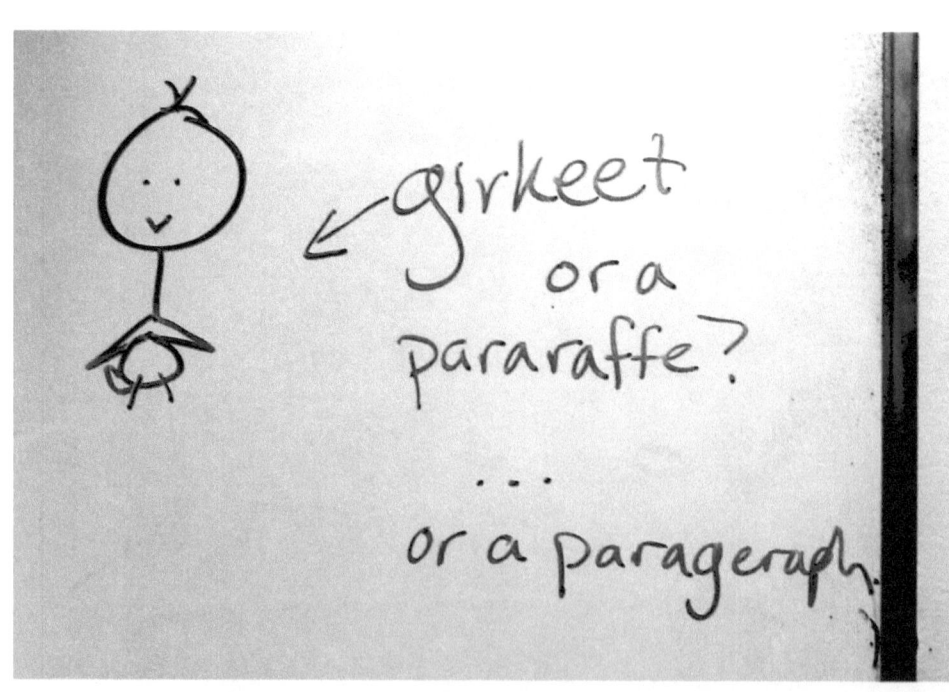

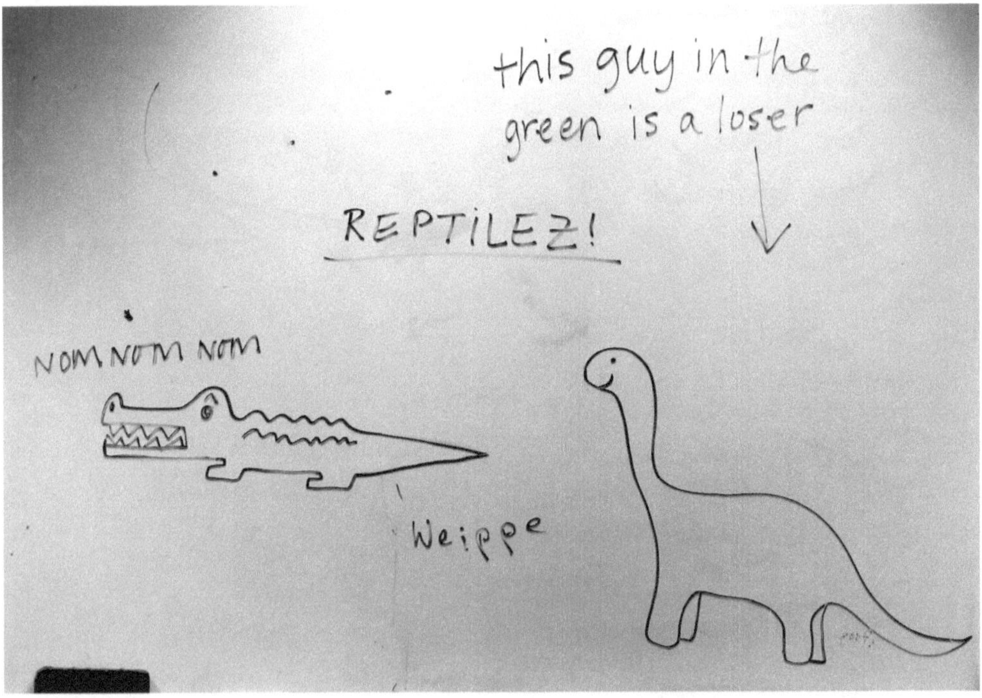
this guy in the
green is a loser
REPTILEZ!
NOM NOM NOM
Weippe

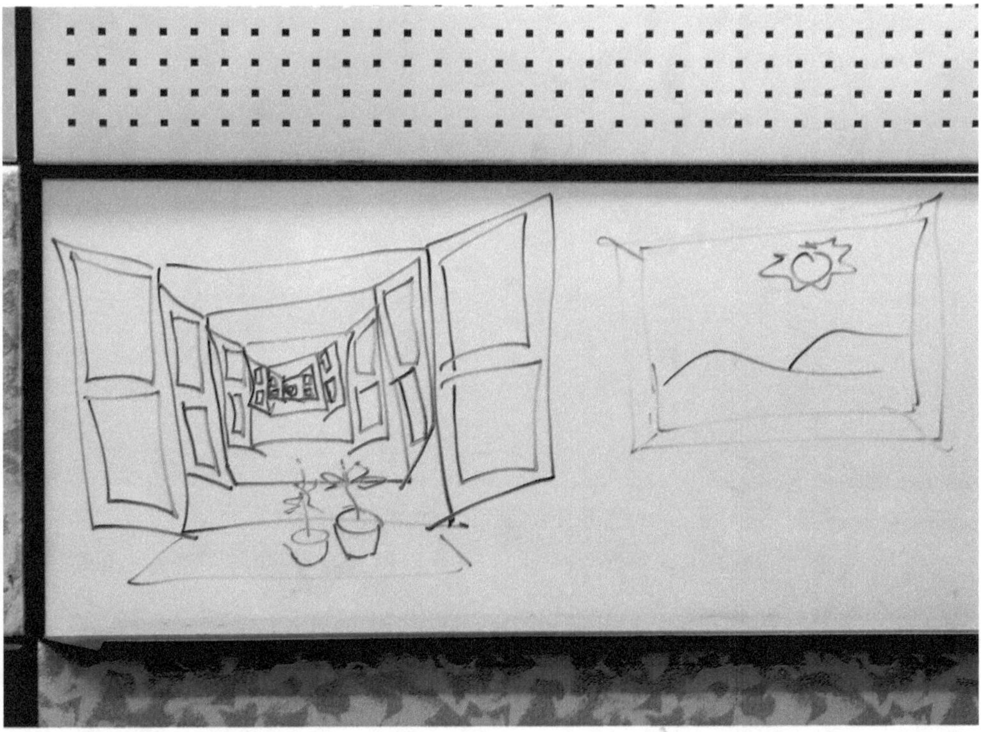

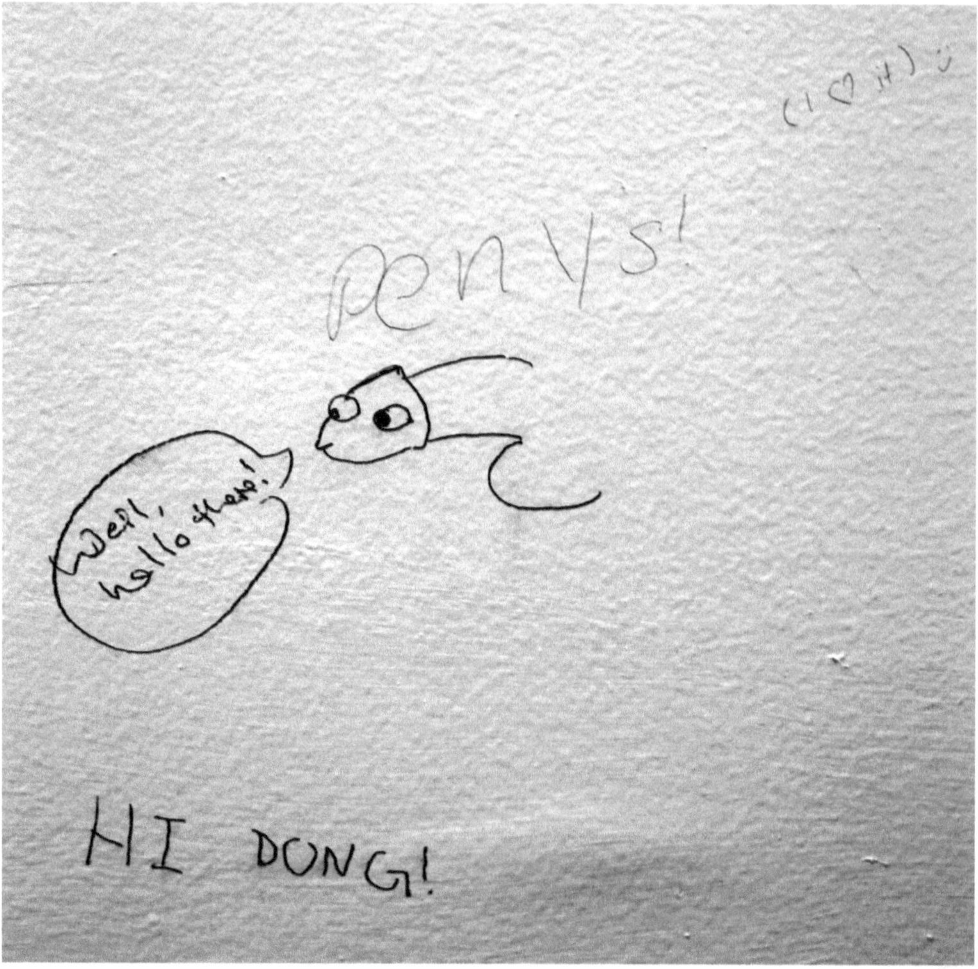
(I ♡ it) :)
penys!
Well, hello there!
HI DONG!

trai(ere)ctory

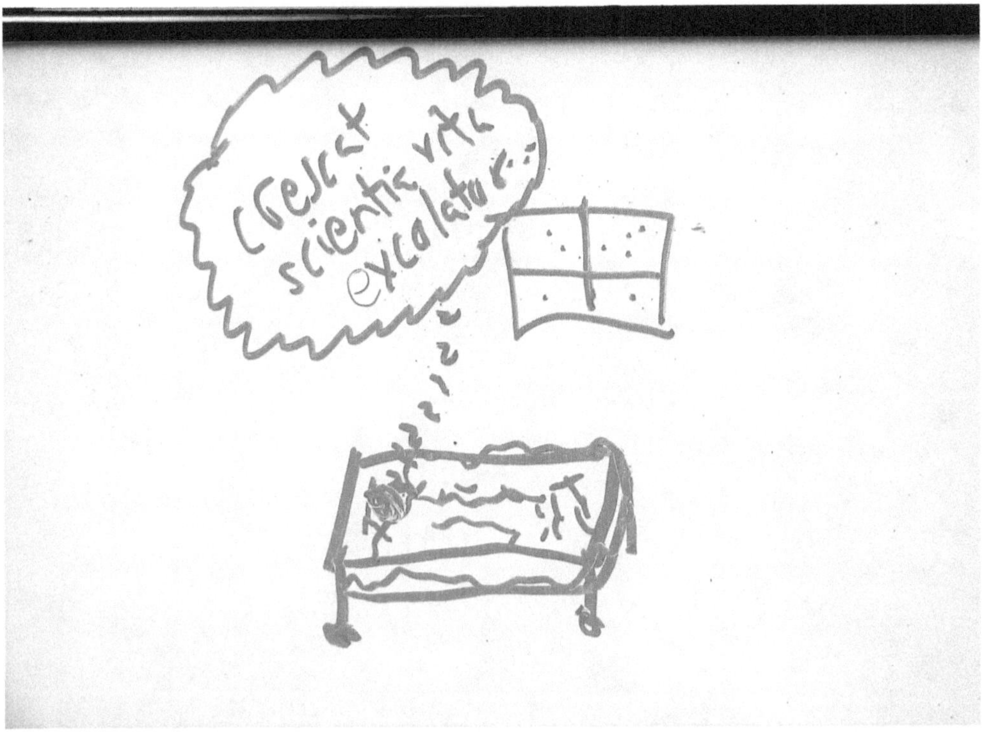

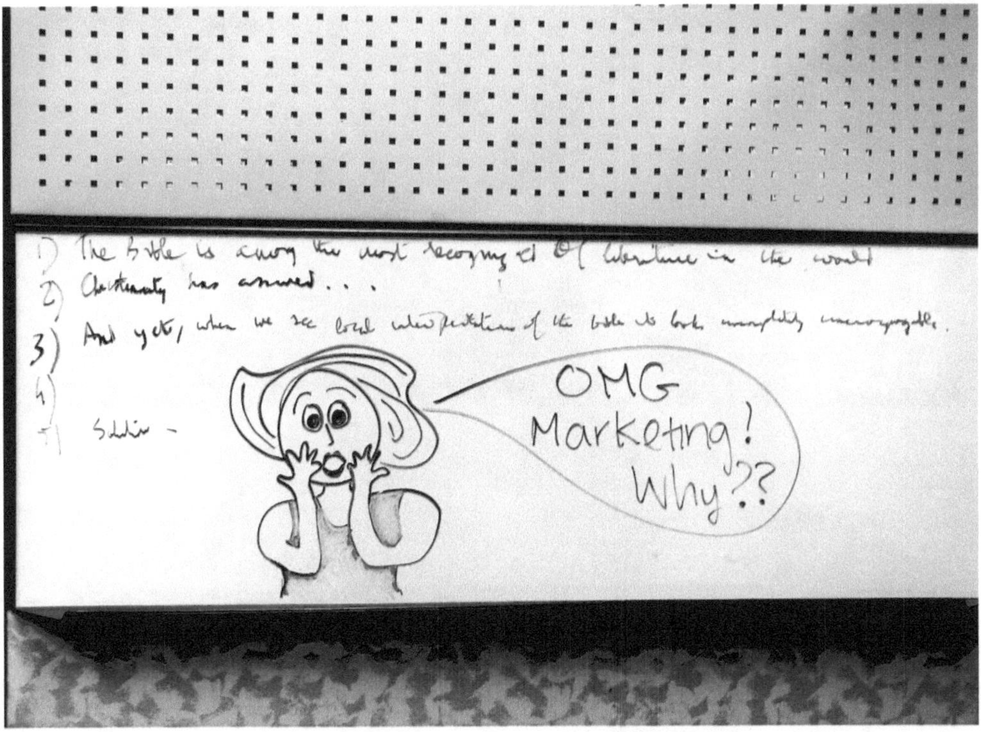
OMG
Marketing!
Why??

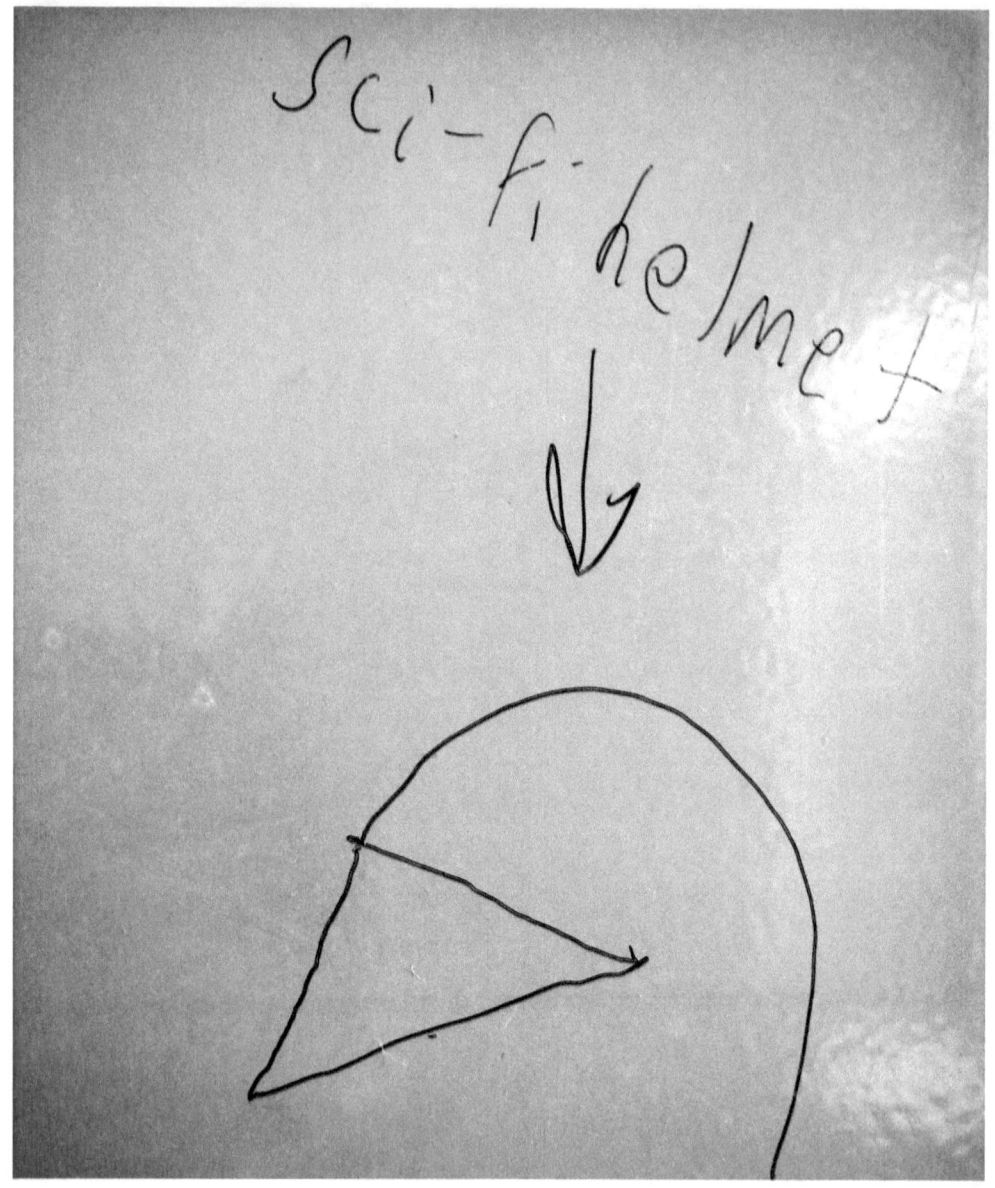

Grades

Why... can't
I get higher
than a B on
a paper?

You should write better

→ I got an
A- once,
Maybe you should
concentrate more
and not write on
walls. It shows you're
distracted

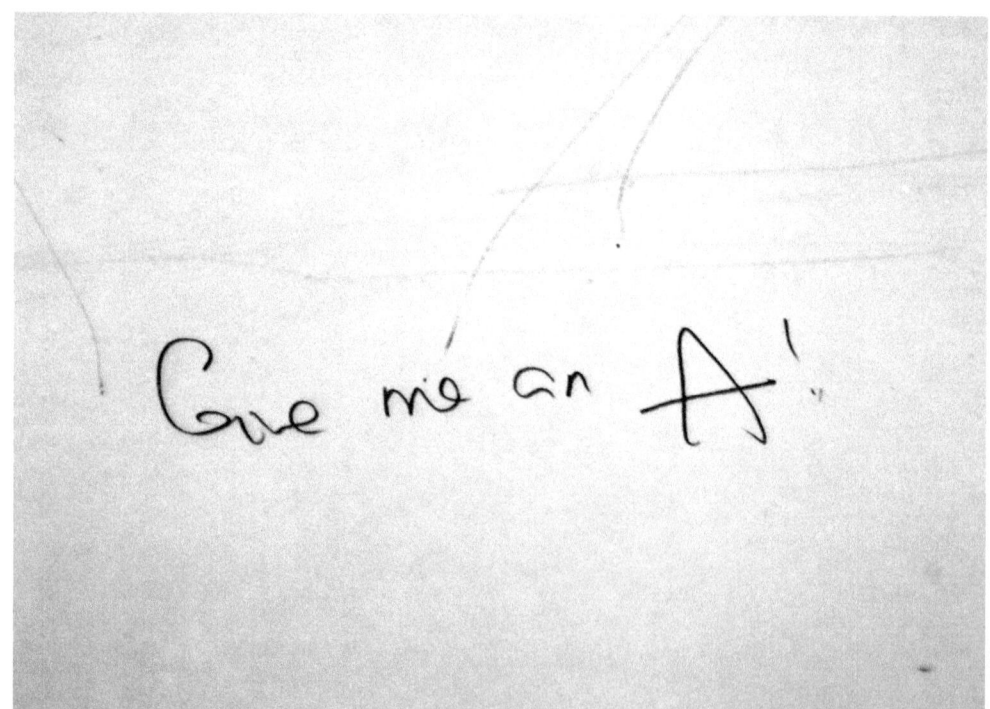

Gue me an A!

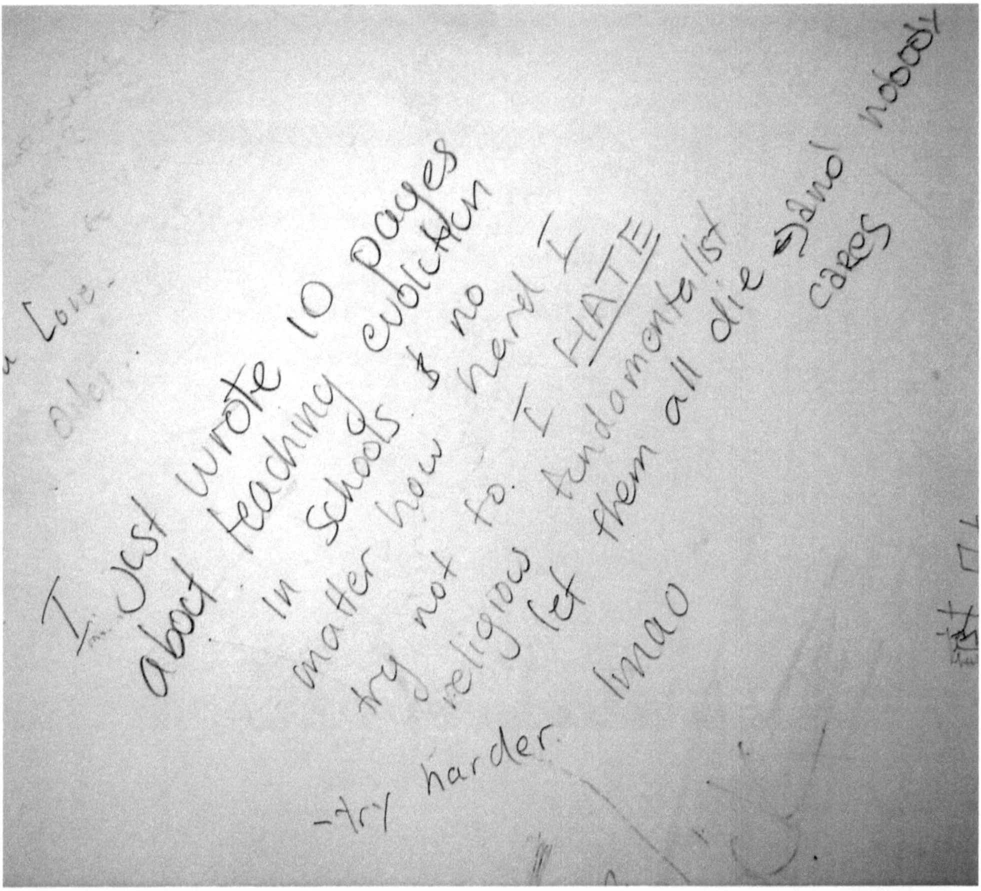

I just wrote 10 pages about teaching evolution in schools & no matter how hard I try not to. I <u>HATE</u> religious fundamentalist let them all die —and nobody cares

-try harder. lmao

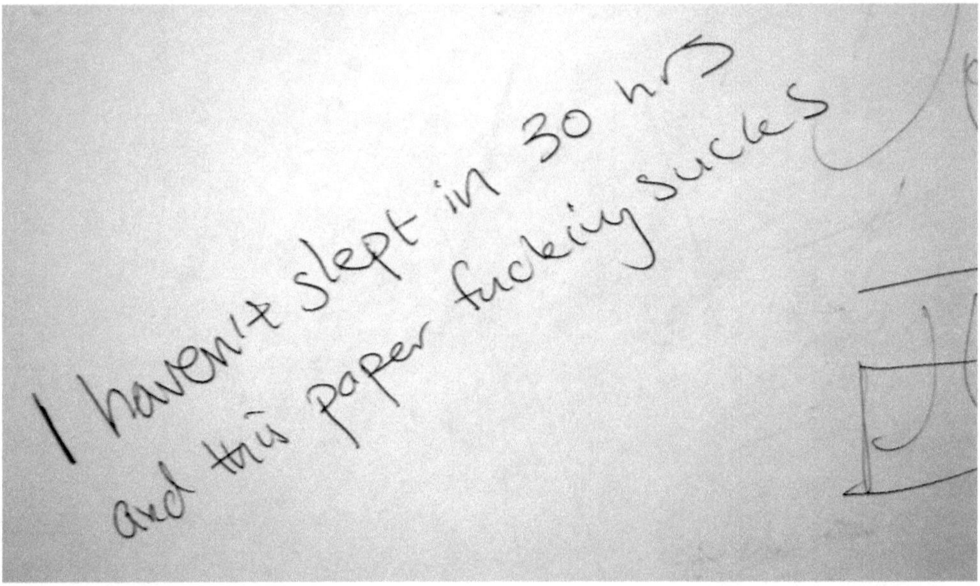

I haven't slept in 30 hrs and this paper fucking sucks

Remember, even if you fail your classes,
at least everybody else is going to drown
with you on this sinking ship.

Bad Grades →
" we don't die,
we multiply! "
FML ☹

BA Papers

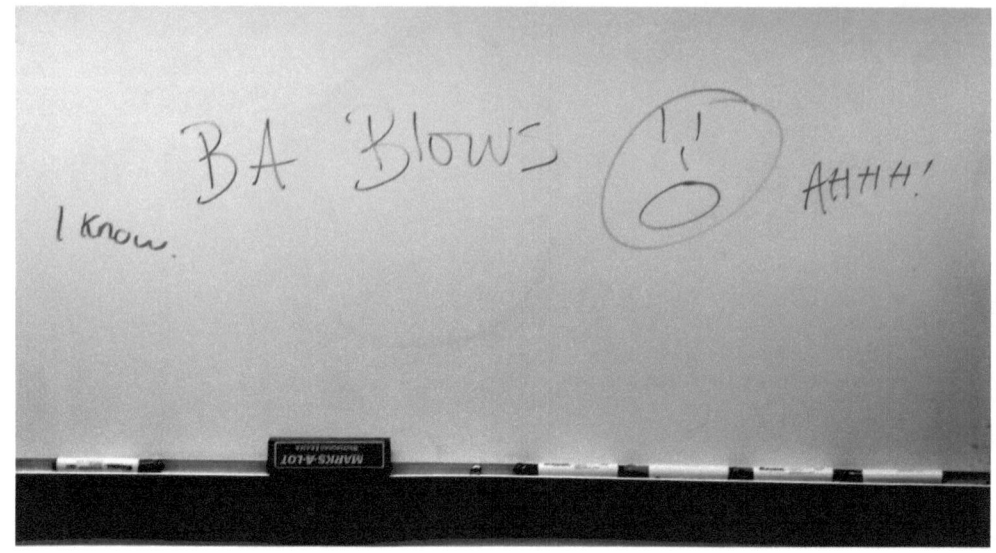

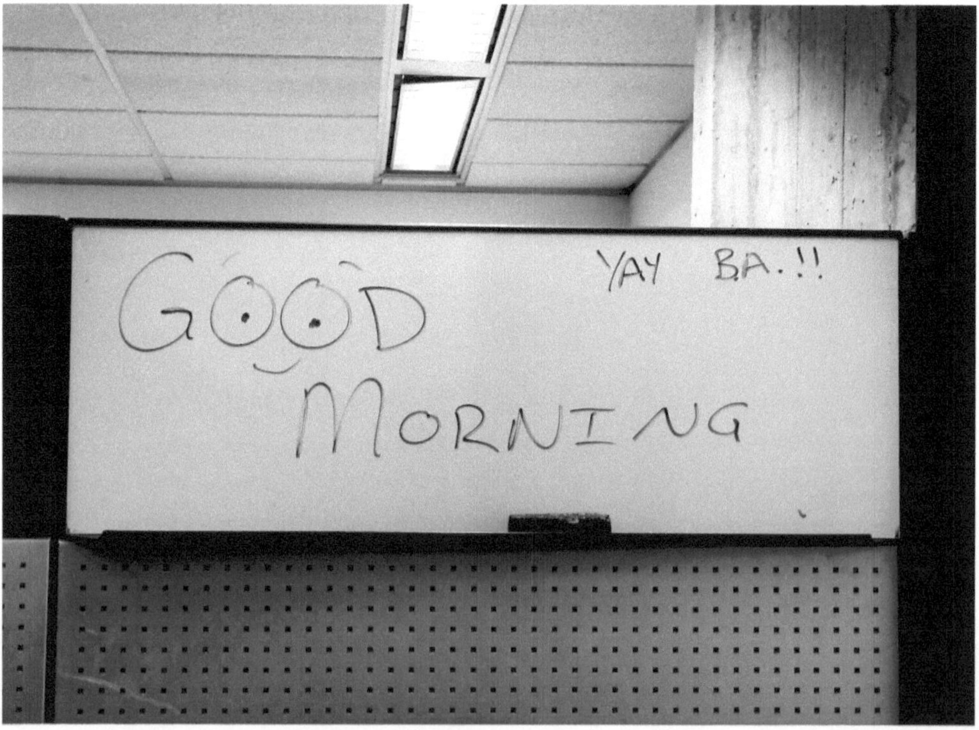

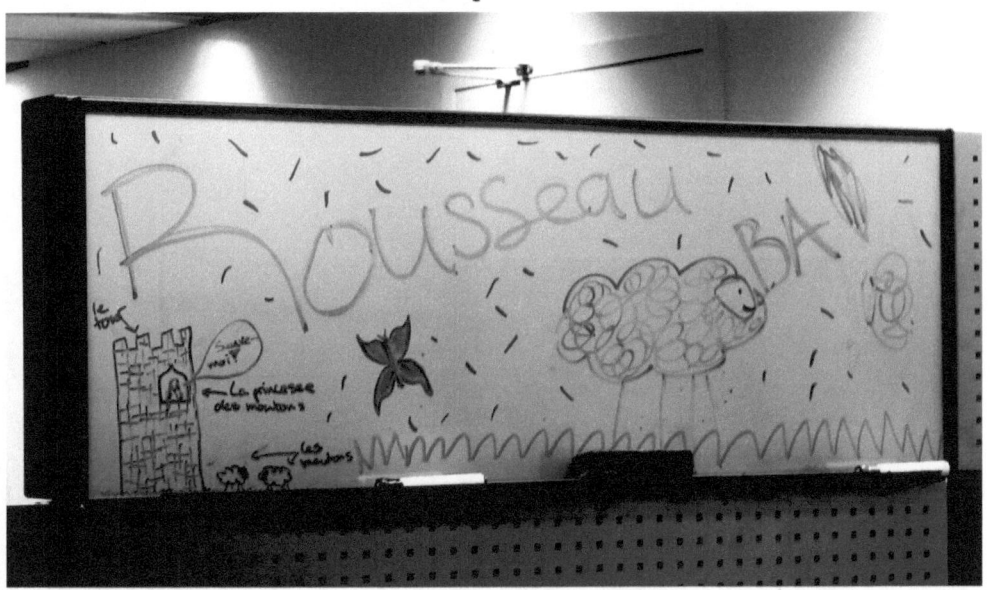

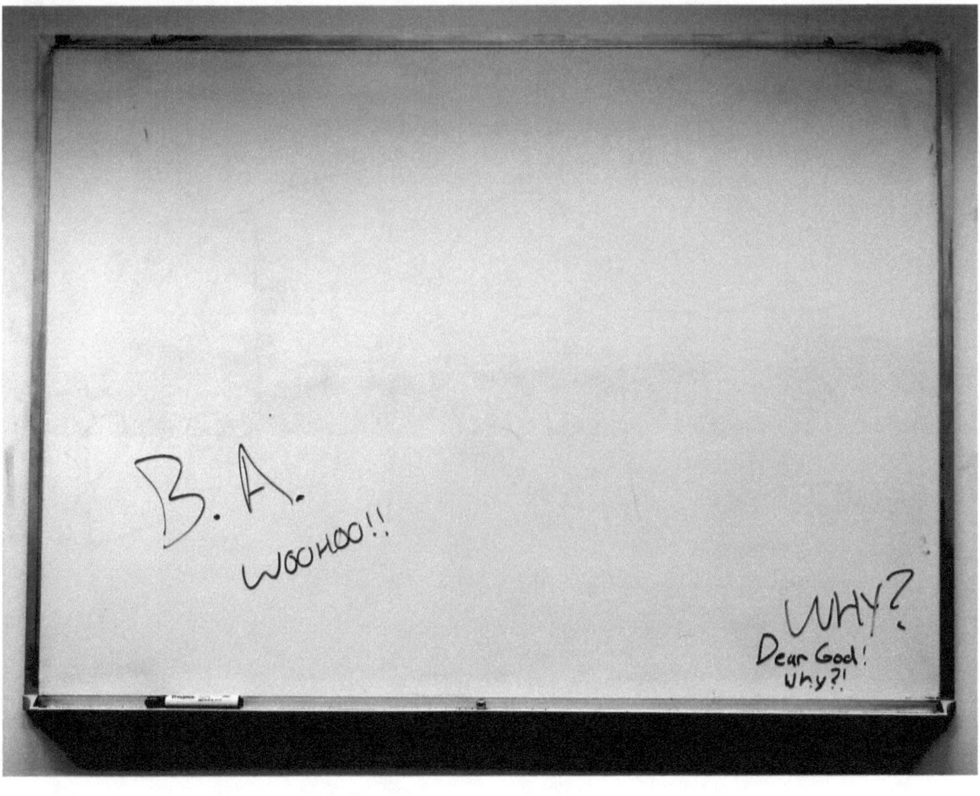

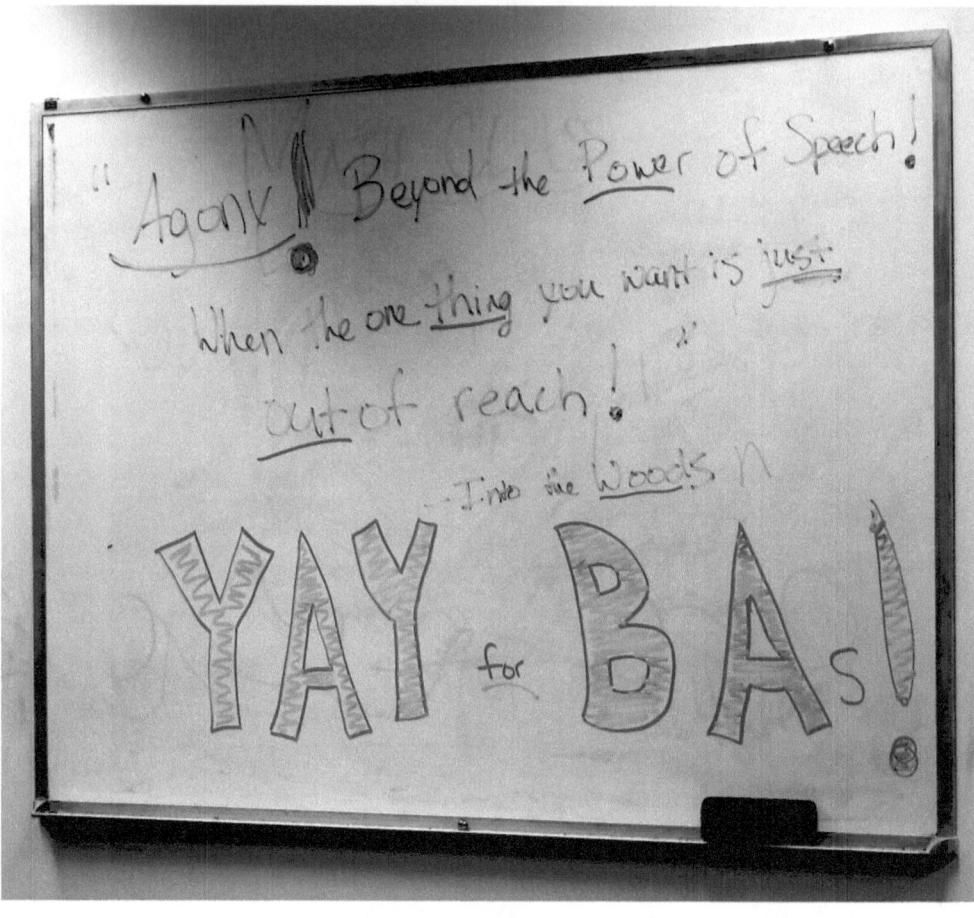

Motivation

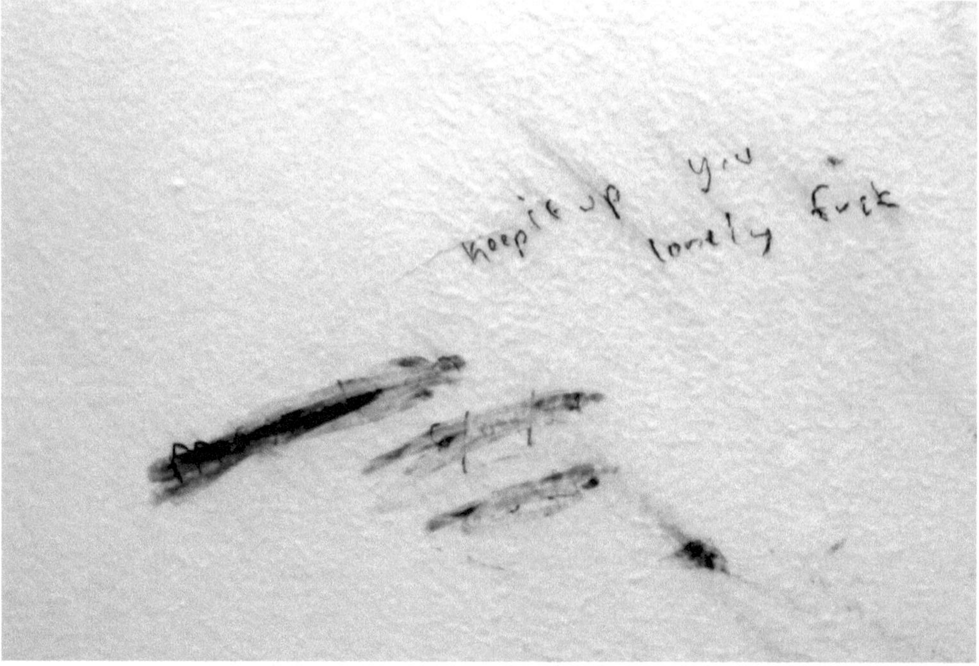

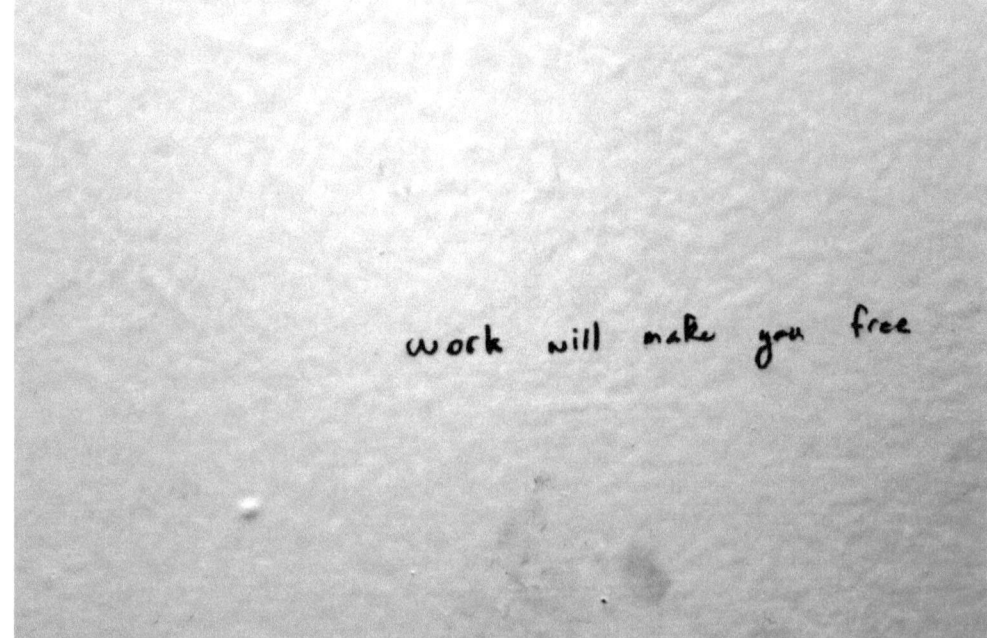

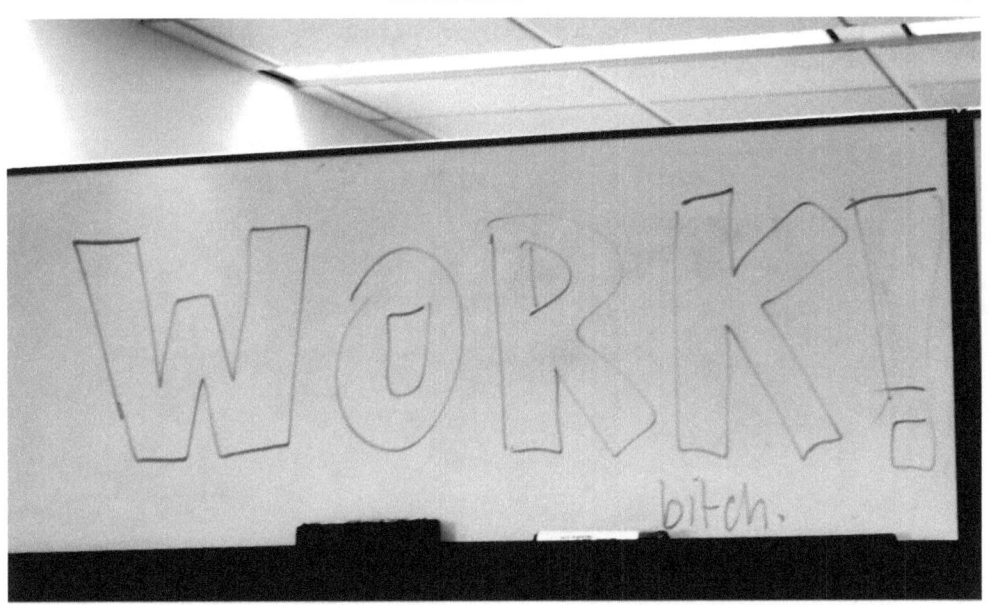

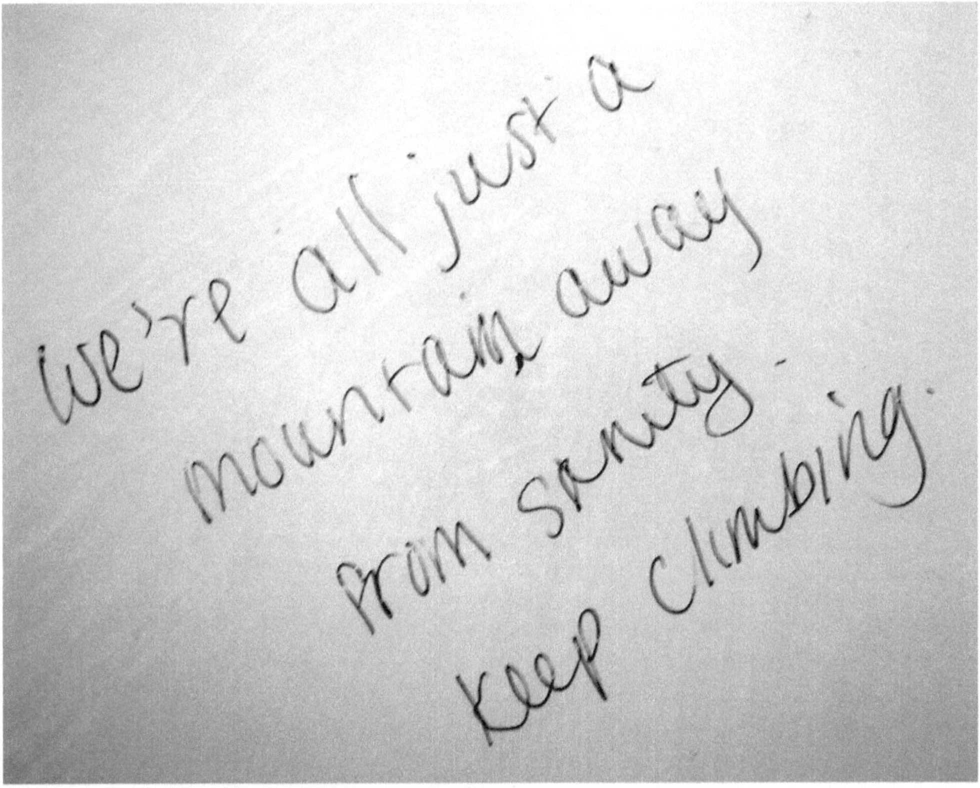

We're all just a mountain away from sanity. keep climbing.

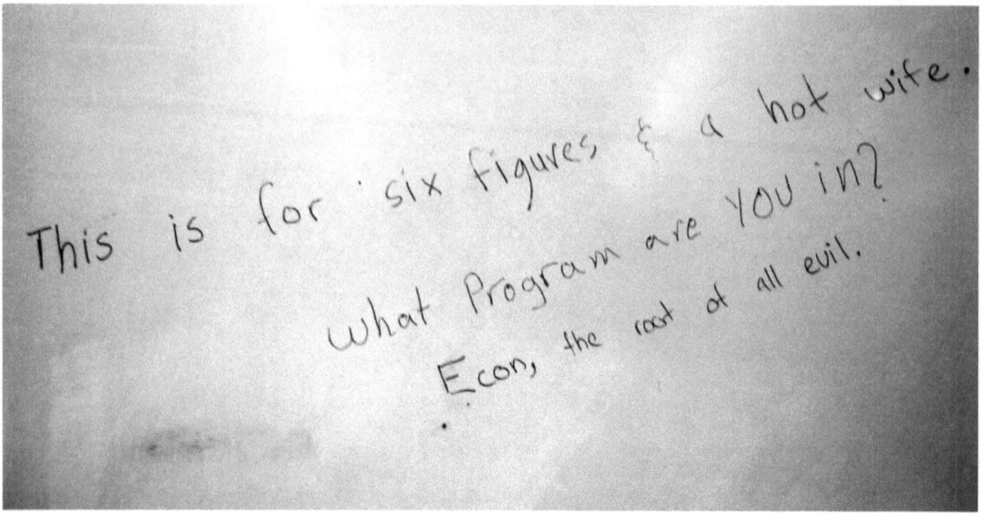

This is for six figures & a hot wife.
What Program are YOU in?
Econ, the root of all evil.

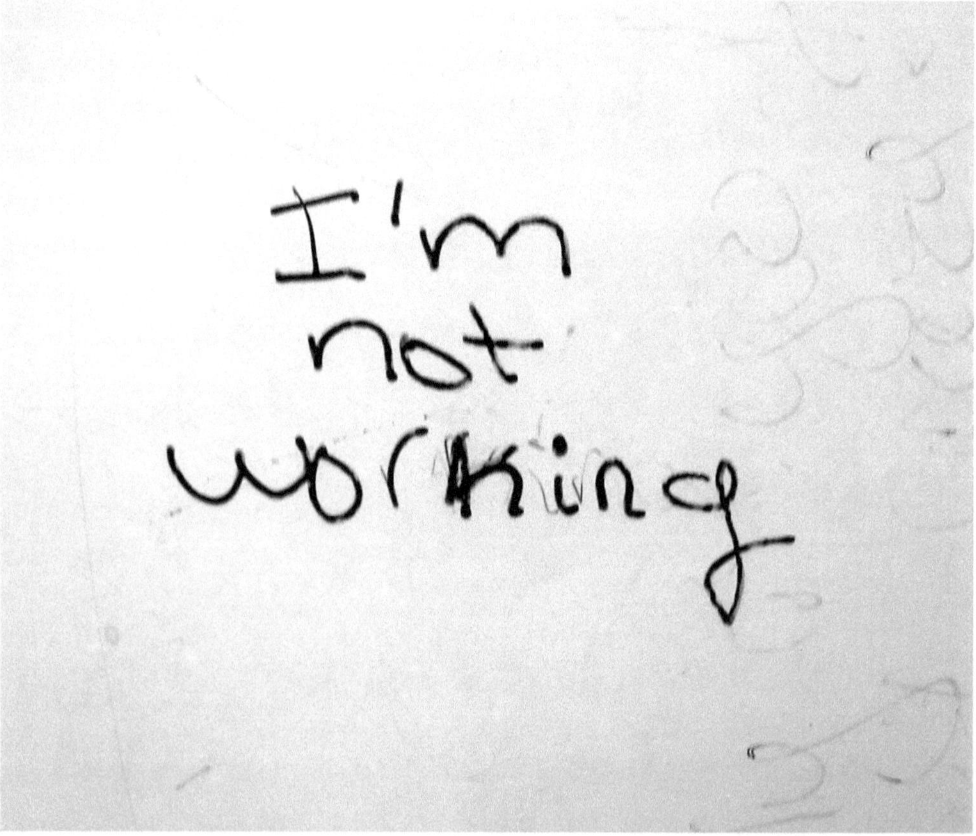

I'm
not
working

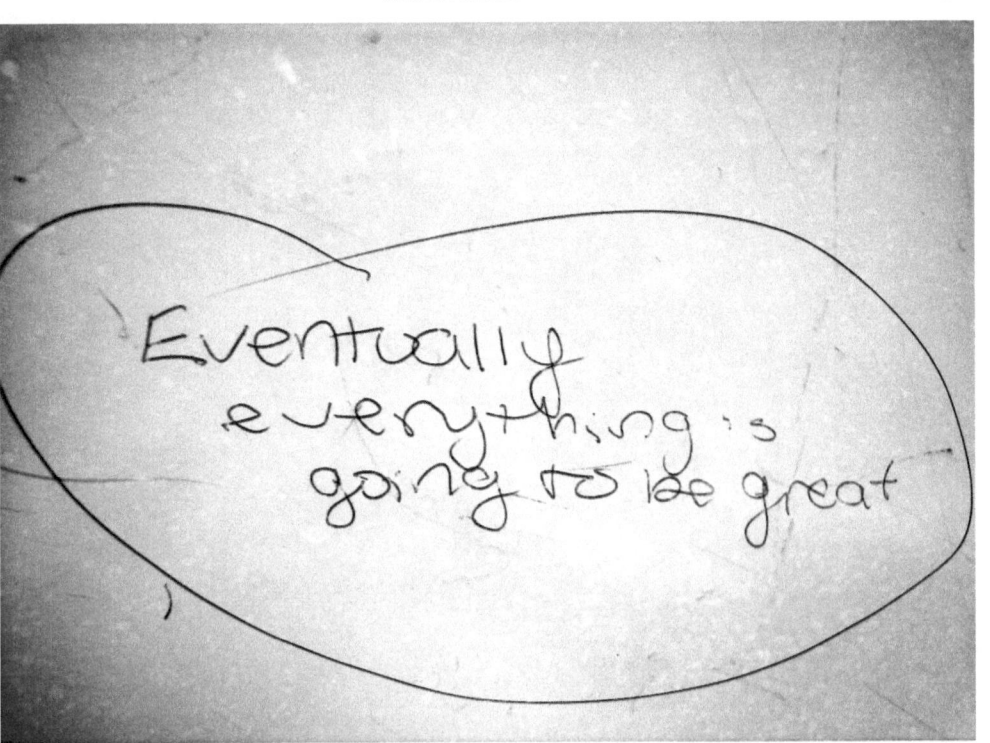

Good luck on whatever brings you here! You can do it! Don't despair!

Thanks!

We're studying hard
Tired little worker bees
for reals yo

It'll be worth it!

everything wanna fall right into place, if we only had a we...
all fall faster everyday ... If only time flew like a dove, will...
it fly faster than I'm falling in love.
he we're not giving up...Let's make it last forever...

GAMING, "HALLELUJAH!"

make it last forever...

STAY   U CAN
              DO IT
AWAKE

goal...page 5...

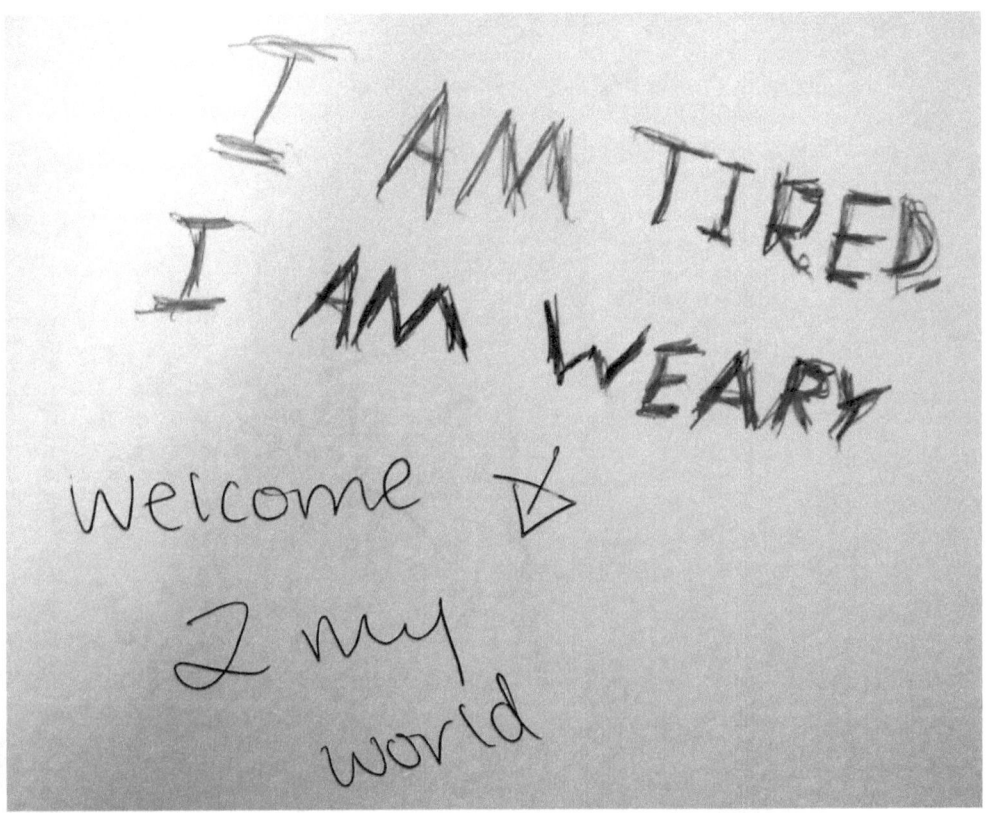

I AM TIRED
I AM WEARY
welcome ▷
2 my
world

why waste
your
life
here?

why
any

Temporary sacrifice
for later reward.

life is hard ... but compared to what?

Quotes

UNCONCERNED, MOCKING VIOLENT—
THUS WISDOM WANTS US: SHE IS A
WOMAN AND ALWAYS LOVES ONLY
A WARRIOR — NILTZCHE misquoted

All things excellent are as difficult as they are rare.
—Some Douche Bag

(Some Douche Bag, more commonly known as Baruch Spinoza.)

The happy life is regarded as a life in conformity with virtue. It is a life which involves effort and is not spent in amusement.
— Aristotle, Nicomachean Ethics

Penis

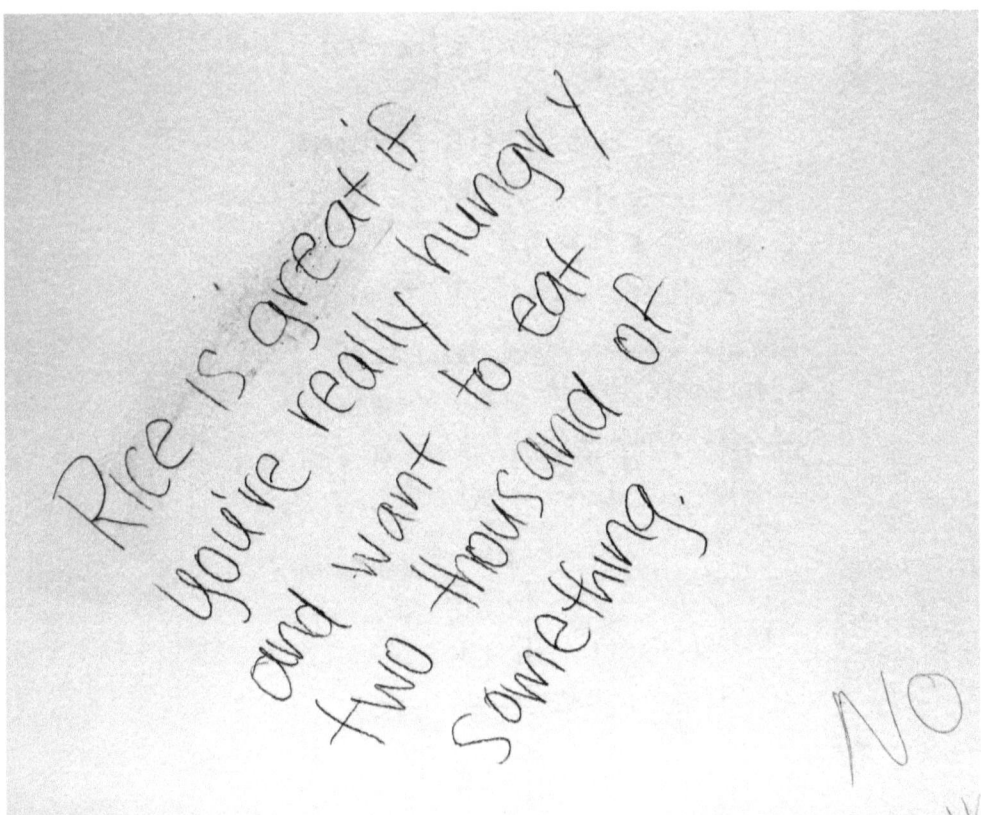

Rice is great if you're really hungry and want to eat two thousand of something.

NO

(Ripoff of Mitch Hedberg.)

Yes, okay — Everyone read this in High School.

Let us go then, you and I
When the evening is spread
out against the sky
Like a patient etherised upon
a table;
Let us go then, through
half deserted streets, The
muttering repeats
Of restless nights in one-night
cheap hotels And sawdust
restaurants with oyster-shells:
Streets that follow like a tedious
argument Of insidious intent
To lead you to an overwhelming
question Oh, do not ask
"What is it?" Let us go
and make our visit.

(The beginning of "The Love Song of J. Alfred Prufrock" by T.S. Eliot)

Time

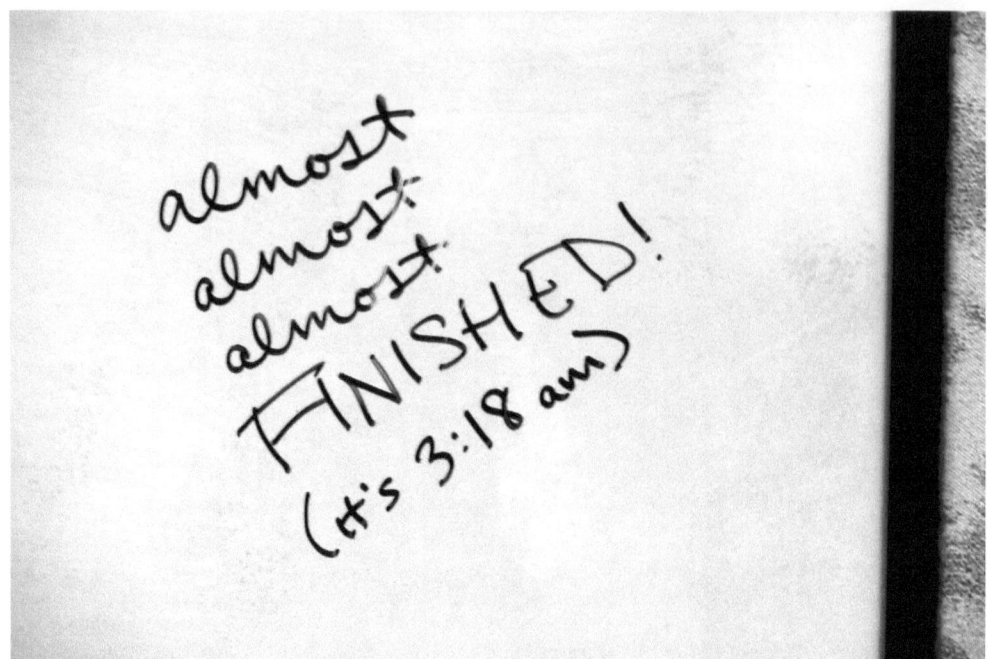

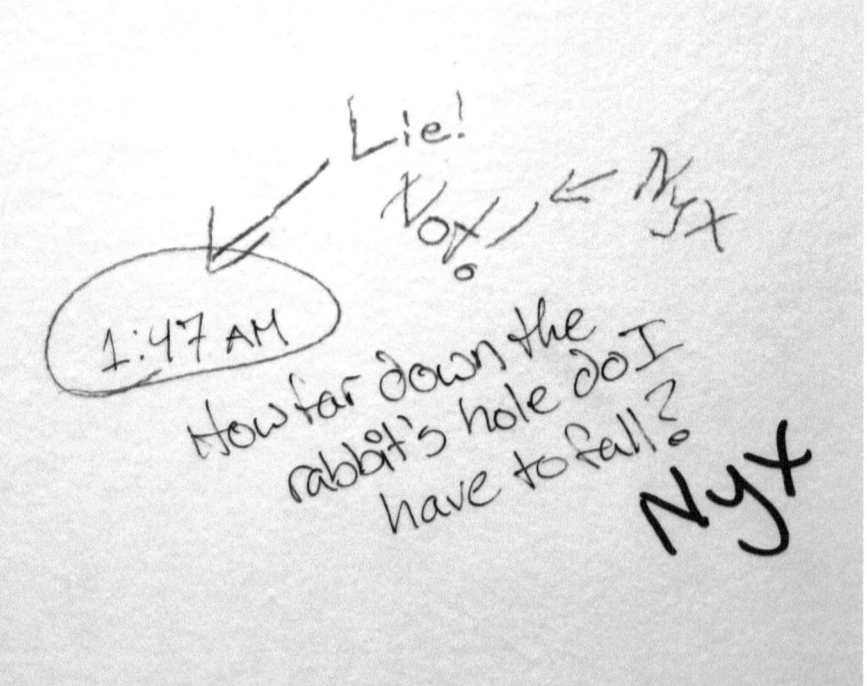

(Note: The part of the library where this is written closes at 1 AM.)

"this would have been better if I did it day by day instead of minute by minute" — ERIN @ 4:50 AM

"My GPA is not high enough to get honors" — Jen
"my GPA is not high enough to work @ a car wash" — Erin

"Jen, I could hear the whistling of your nose" — Erin

"pupu, caca" — Esmeralda

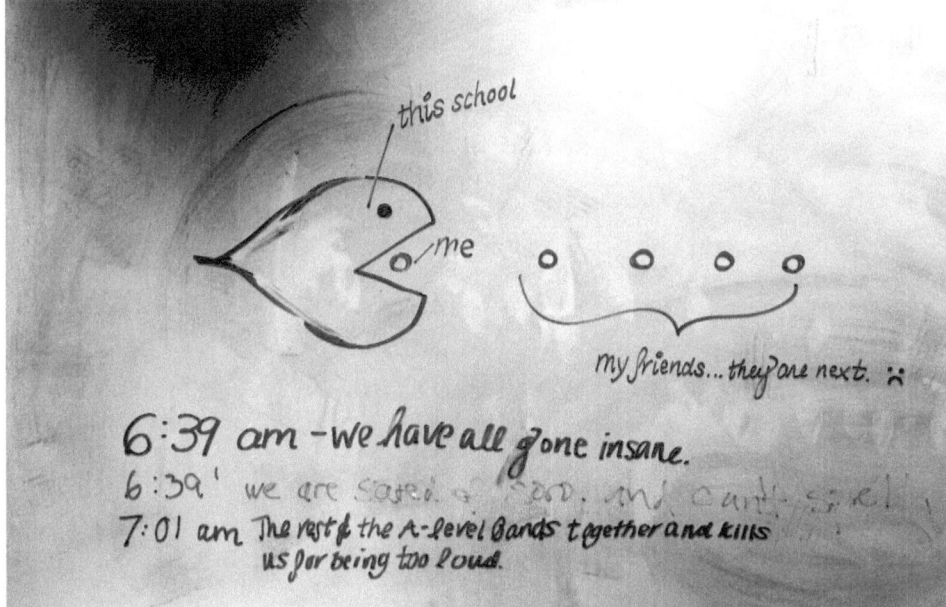

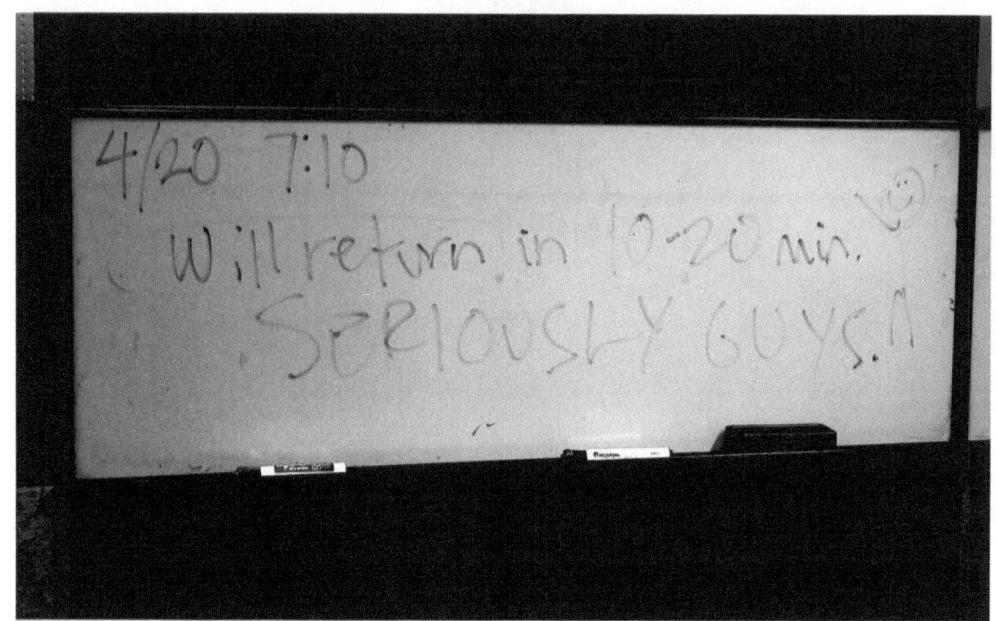

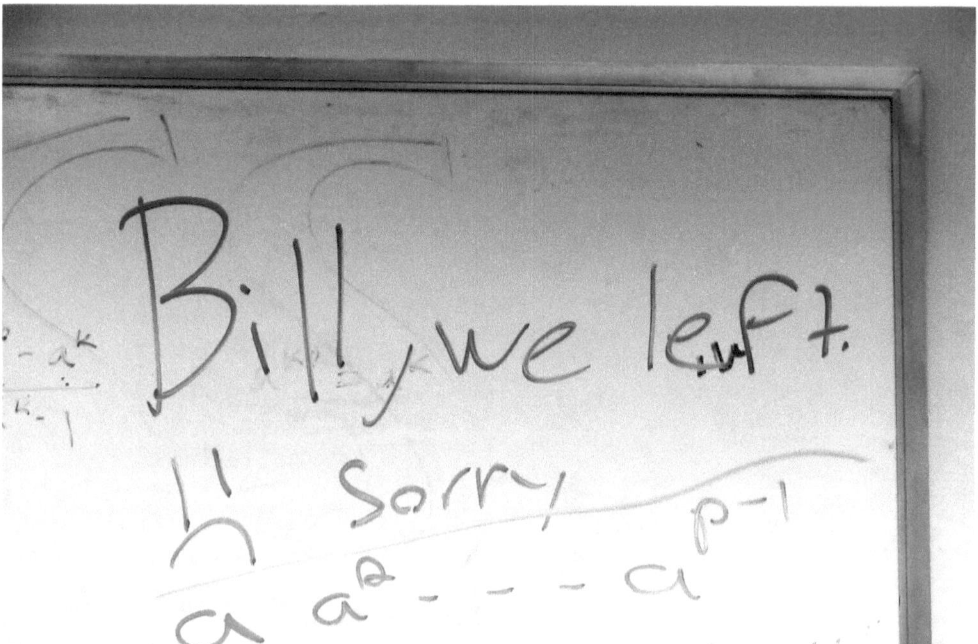

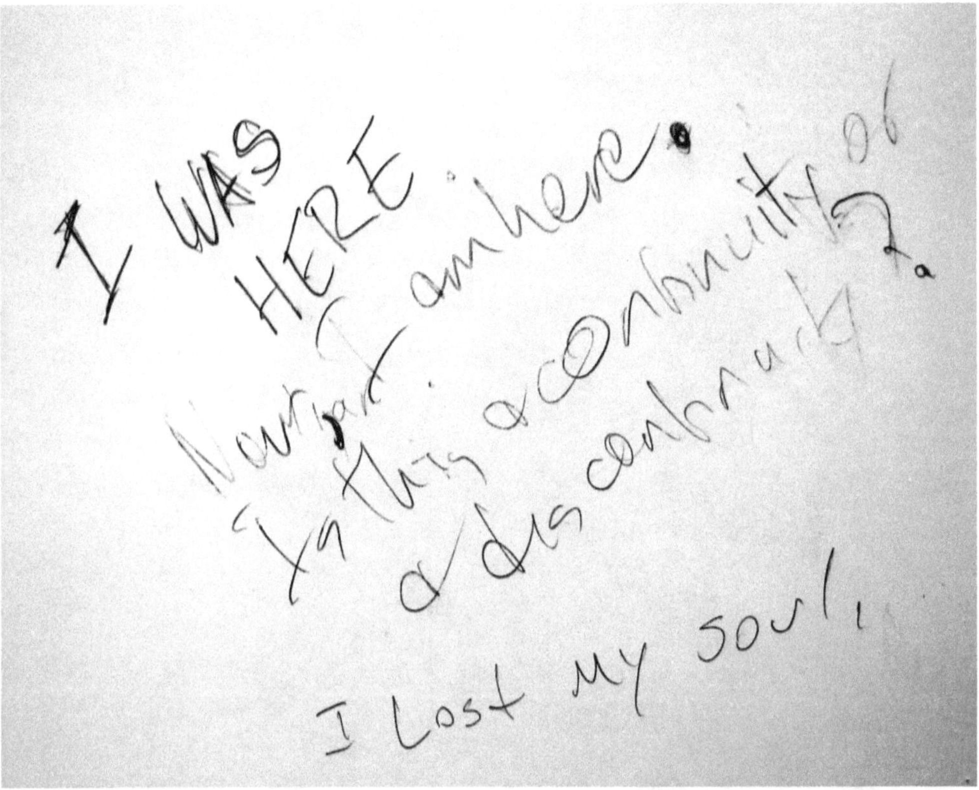

I WAS HERE.

Now I am here.

Is this a continuity of 06
a father discontinuity?

I Lost My soul,

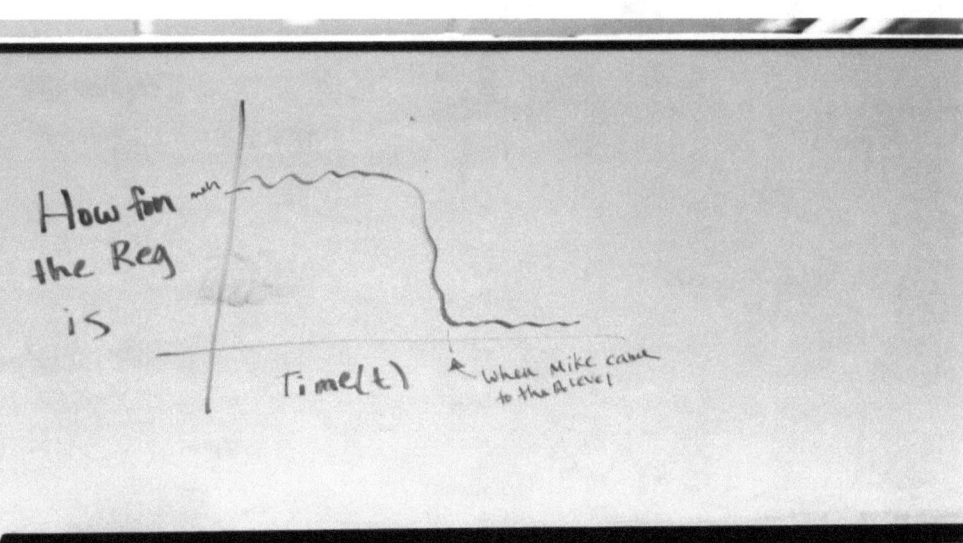

How fun the Reg is

Time(t)

← When Mike came to the 4 level

```
10:40  ps 119
11:50  ps 150
1:00   ps 150
                      1:15   ps 15
                      3:30   ps 65

                      5:00   ps 100
                      6:00   ps 130
```

with the
    avg lifespan
today, you only
have about 55
more years...
good thing you
are getting such
a good education

Wordplay

5th FLOOR, BREAKER OF SoulS.
Pierce. Anal exploder.

(Pierce is a student dormitory: http://en.wikipedia.org/wiki/Pierce_Tower)

Buttflakes
Haunt my dreams
like Snow Flakes Fall in
winter

GAH!
HAG!

Hello
O, HELL!

Write your name if you are a poet.
Homer   Shakespeare
HORACE
SAPPHO
R.L. Dante

I'm broke as hell
but I'm not dead yet

My dick burns like hell
I think it's broke.

Winter is the suck
Internships, schoolwork, No sun
Spring will melt it all

가득비ᄀ

Poopy McPoop was a
happy fellow...
He was plea salt and
Affably mellow.
Until one sad day
Someone flushed him away.
My goodness how poopy
did bellow!

"This has no meaning you, said
some boring fucking kid with his head
So far up his bum
That he rags on dumb fun
To feel big, though he's spiritually dead.

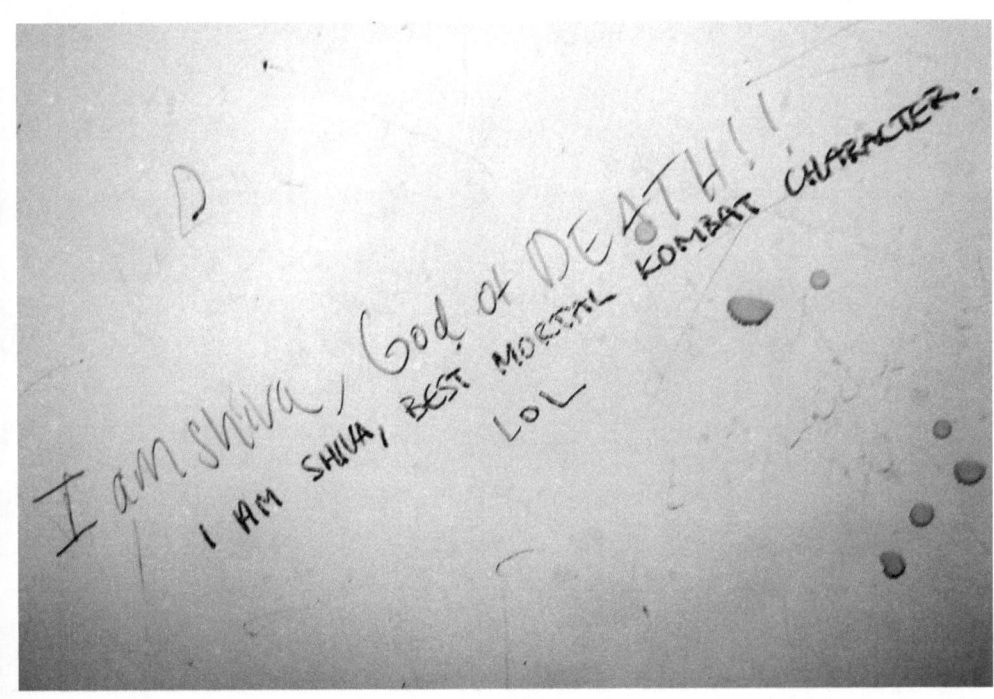

D

I am shiva, God of DEATH!!
I AM SHIVA, BEST MORTAL KOMBAT CHARACTER.
LOL

booze
booze
you make me love
but now I win
drunk as Hunk Finn!
In 5 weeks I cruise (typo intentional)

INSIDE THE WALLS OF PRISON MY BODY MAY BE
BUT THE LORD HAS SET MY SOUL FREE
Alas, For trapped in Hyde Park still is thee

(Spinoff of Johnny Cash's "Greystone Chapel")

Orthography

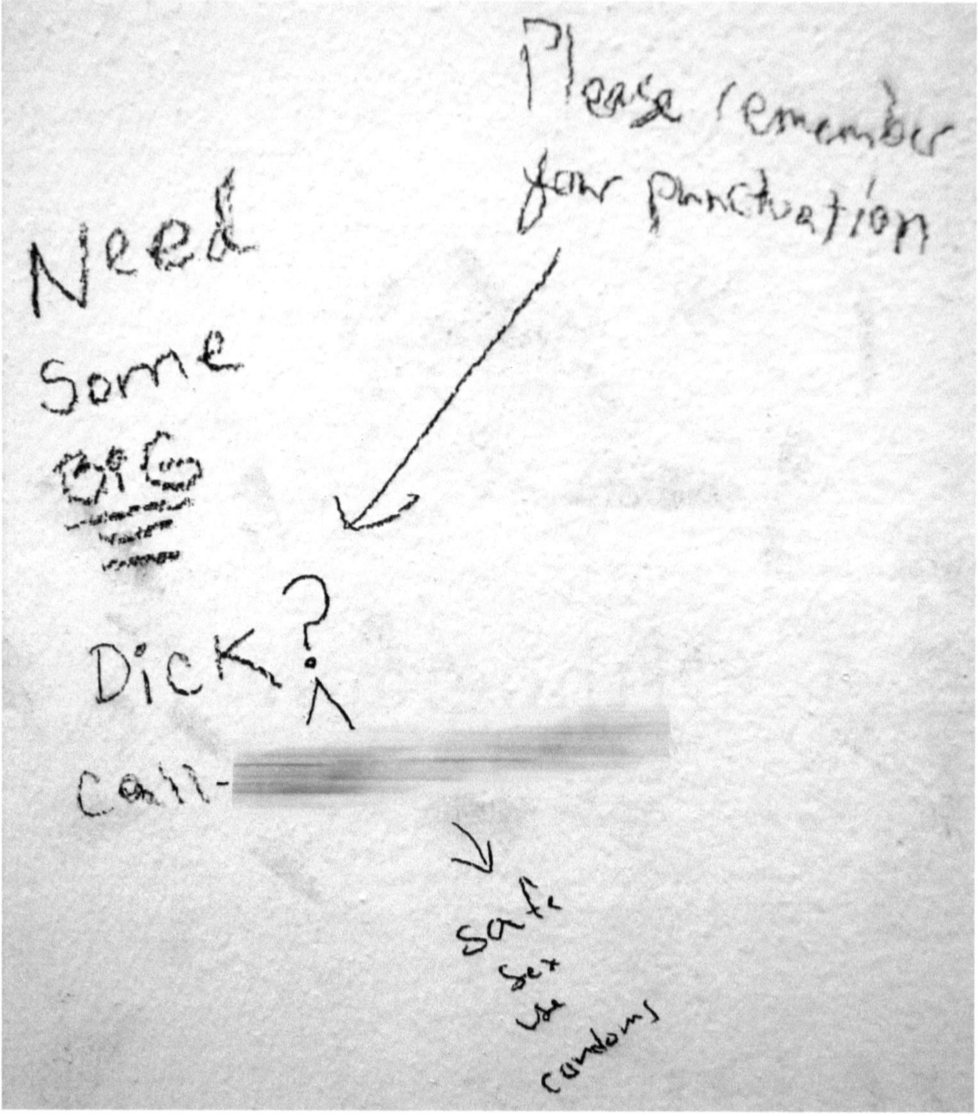
Please remember your punctuation
Need
Some
Dick?
Call-
safe sex use condoms

TO DO

- Read and "judge".
- Organize "Oral" history thing.
- Find a real end to the "conclusion".
- Continue "fixing" the references.
- Make the "bibliography".

He who sits
here and studies
for an exam,
shall ace it.

"Were true"
↓ subjunctive. Yo

I wish that
was true!

Thanks

it
IS...

YOU RULE!

Entirely True

12:25am
political theory dance parties
in the stacks make
it so much easier to care
about political theory.
try it.

Nyx

↑

would benefit this school

by transferring

↑

would benefit this school
by removing stick from ass
and also maybe learning to spell

↑

would benefit this school
by writing on more walls

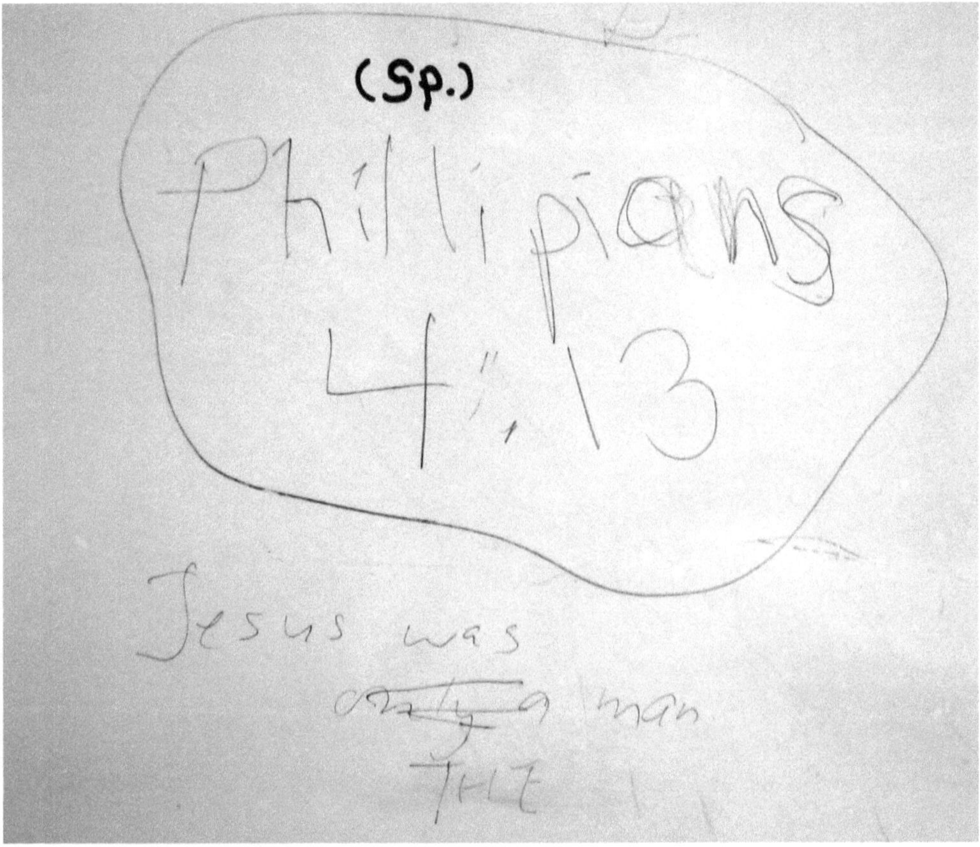

(Sp.)

Phillipians

4:13

Jesus was
~~only~~ a man
THE

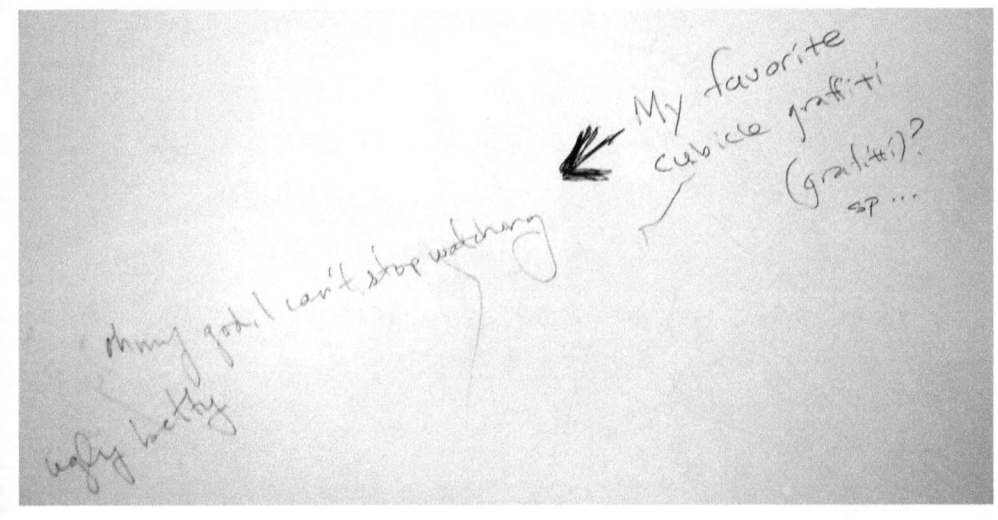

My favorite
cubicle graffiti
(graf(it))?
sp...

ohmy god, I can't stop watching

ugly betty

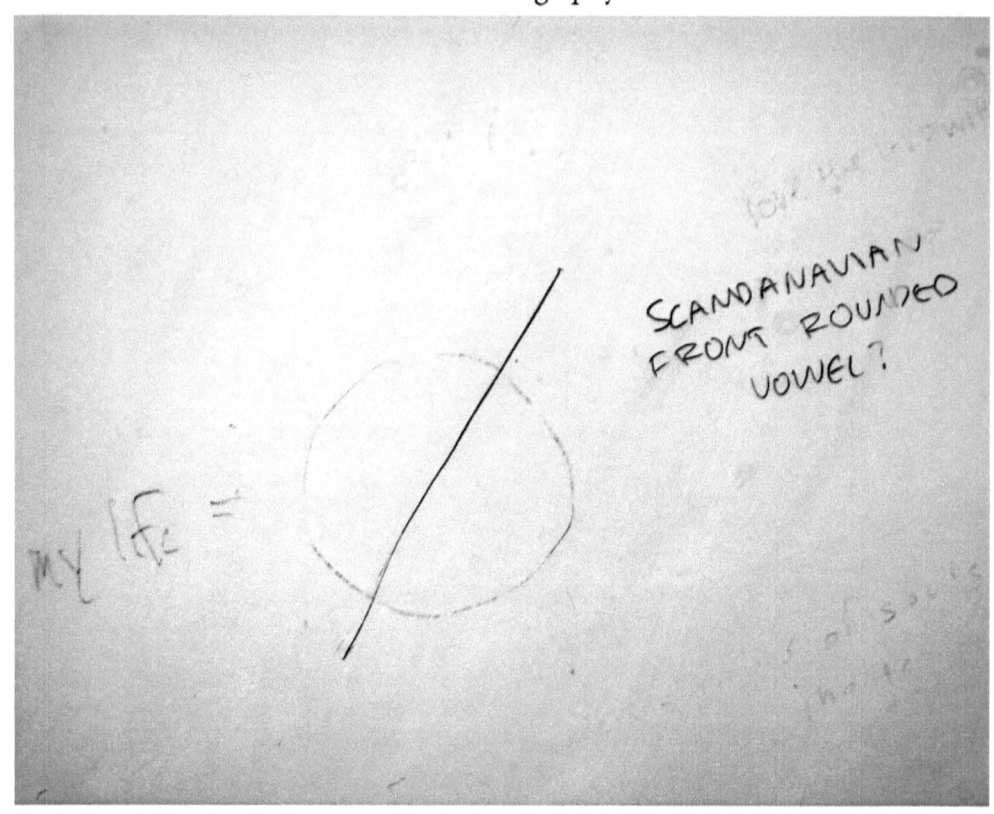

Discussions

I'm sorry for whatever I did to you.
I'm so sorry. Please forgive me.

And you are?
The person who thought we were friends...
Oooh... Being all crispie and stuff...
Do you still come here and think of our wistful memories?
Maybe... Since I don't know who you are, I can't answer your question

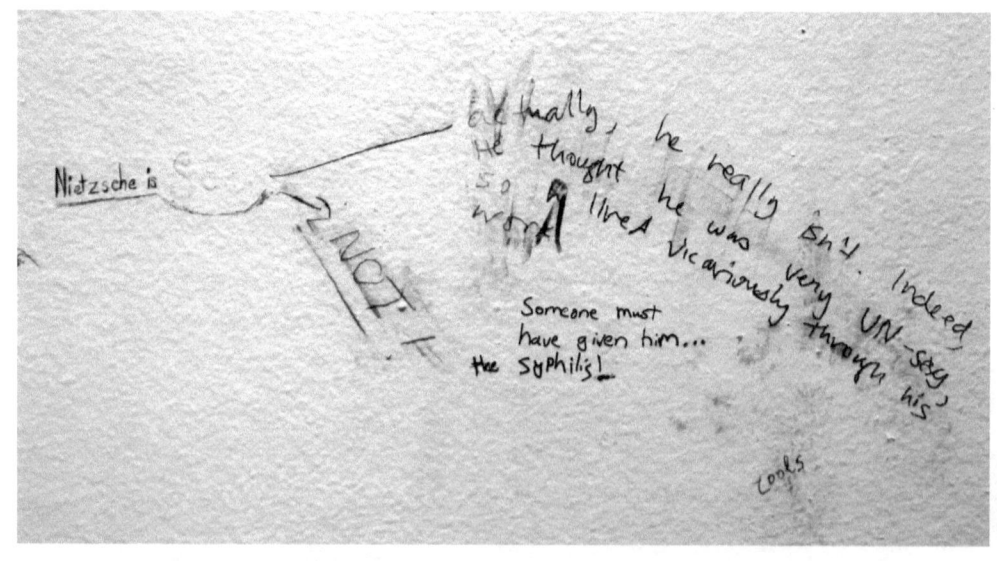

Nietzsche is

NOT!

Actually, he really shit. Indeed,
He thought he was very UN-sexy
So I lived vicariously through his
word

Someone must
have given him...
the syphilis!

cools

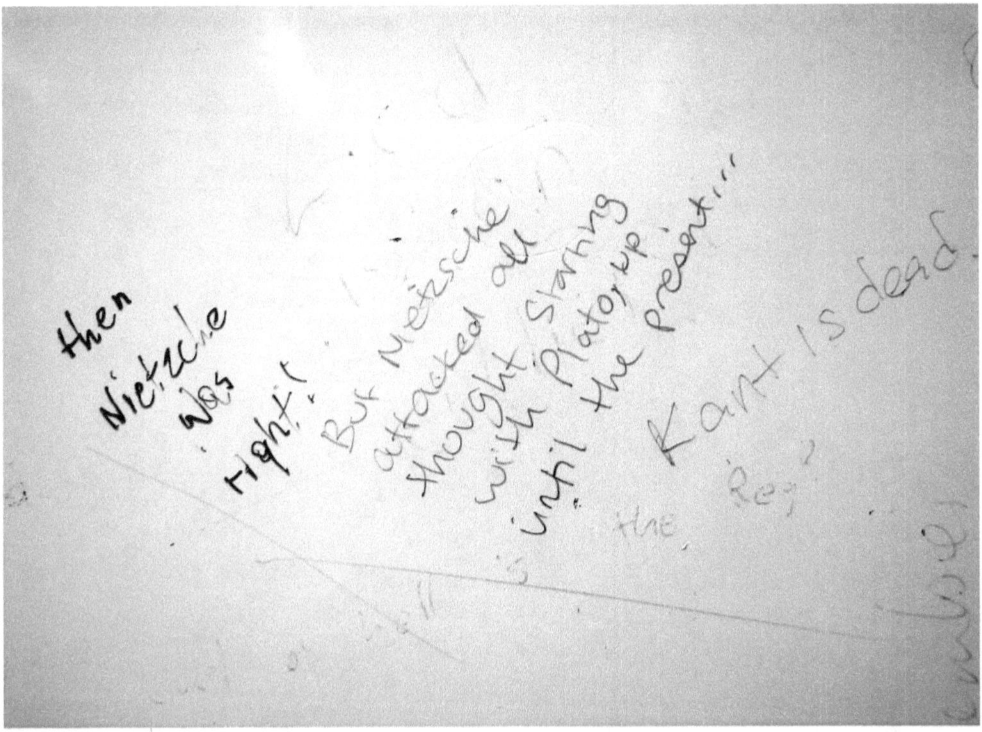

then Nietzsche was right.

But Nietzsche attacked all thought, starting with Plato, right up until the present...

the Reg?

Kant is dead.

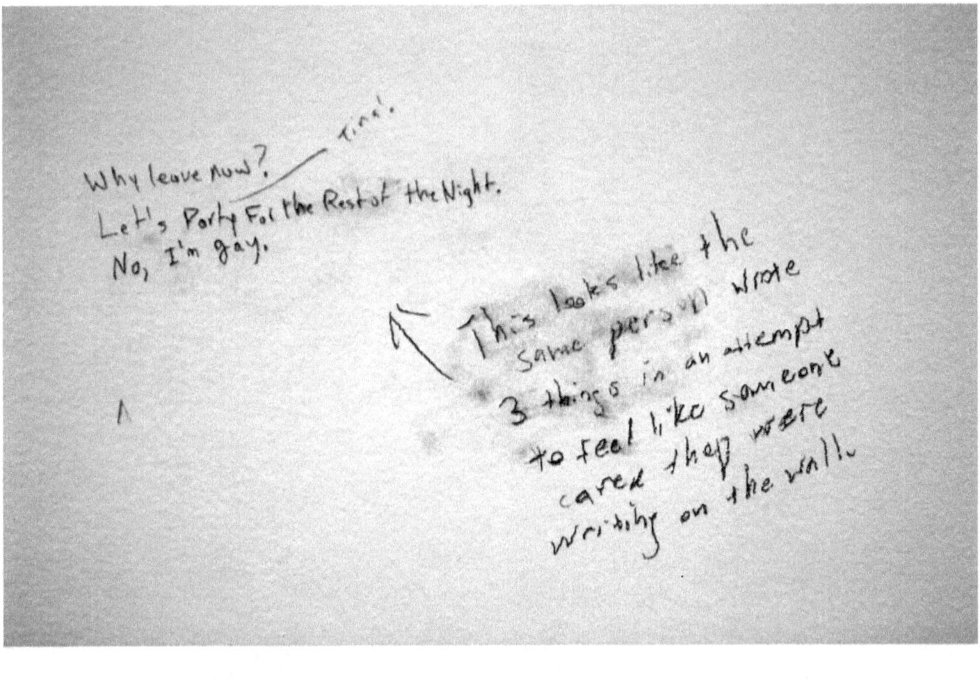

Why leave now? Tim!
Let's Party For the Rest of the Night.
No, I'm gay.

This looks like the same person wrote 3 things in an attempt to feel like someone cared they were writing on the wall.

What have I done? You wrote on a wall.

what they wanted you to

On what you wanted to do

what did they do to you? everything.

how can you ever know?

I wish someone would save me

I wish uchicago was warm.

Bora Bora...
A place so good they named it twice.

I wish I didn't have to convince myself to not to kill myself.

I wish you'd take your head out of your ass, laugh about something, and realize things aren't so tough

you too! (lol)

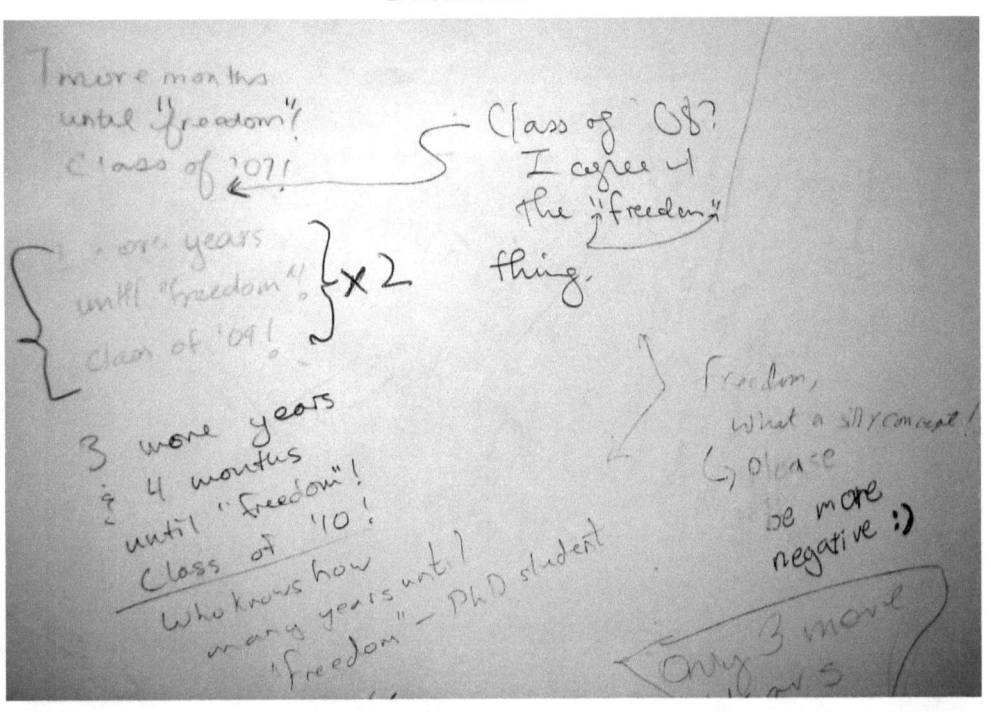

No one knows what I've done.
— Heller, Joe

Santa knows.

Yes, Hedges.

I fucked your mother last night.
Did you know that?
(in the ass) I know you did,
I was the one
videotaping...

Kill me ! → →

HANNAH
AND   ST. PATTY'S
                                DAY
ALICIA
              HAVE SMALL T's
are lesbos
     is an island
     in Greece. No, he means they carpet munch.

This is like prison wall graffiti.
                                    IHT IIHT IHT
Have you been incarcerated?
              Feels like it...

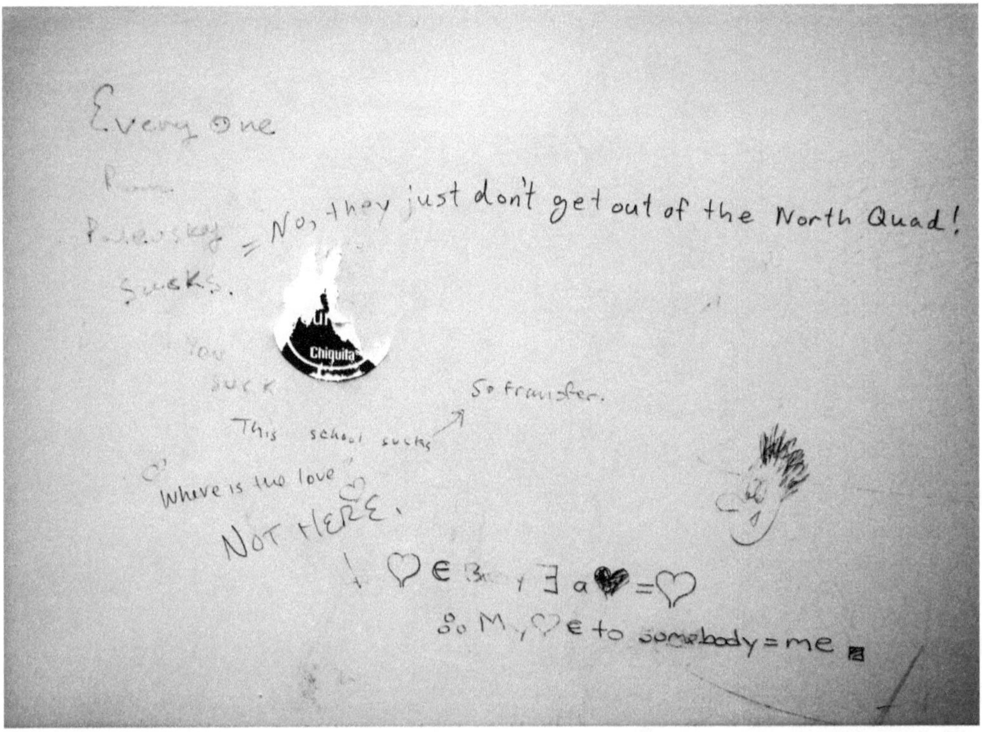

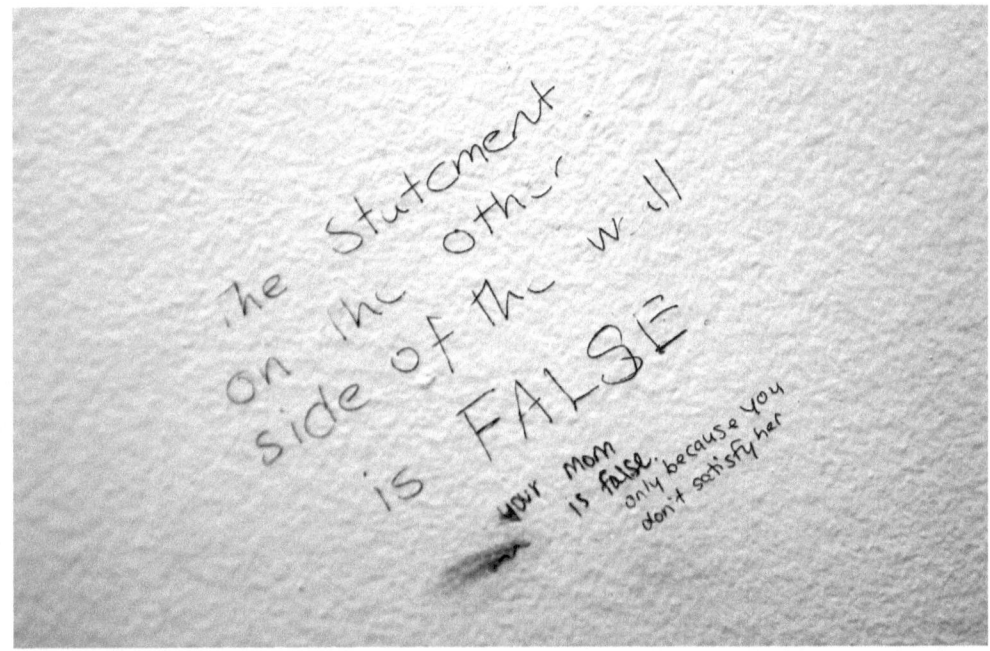

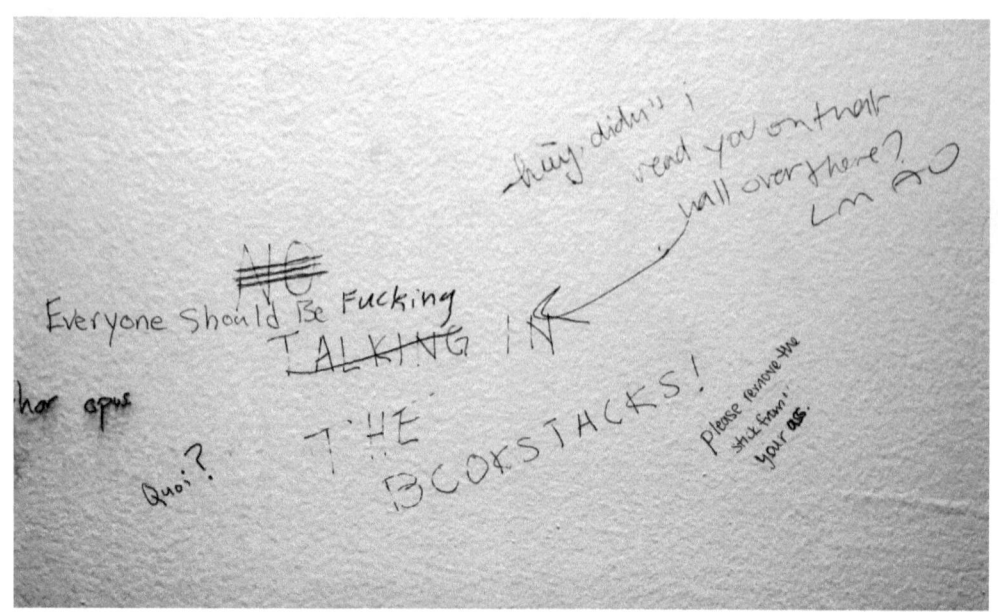

hey, didn't i read you on that wall over there? Lm ao

NO

Everyone Should Be Fucking TALKING IN

hor opus

Quoi?

THE BOOKSTACKS!

Please remove the stick from your ass.

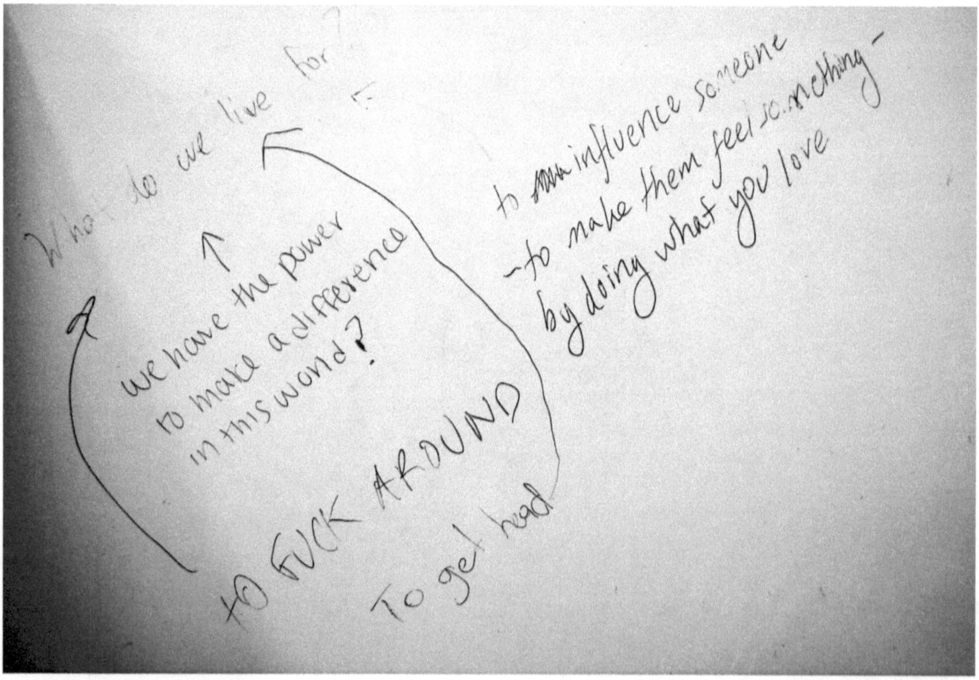

Who do we live for?

we have the power to make a difference in this world?

to influence someone
—to make them feel something—
by doing what you love

TO FUCK AROUND

To get head

FAQ

What's the deal with the book title? And 'graffiti' isn't a Latin word!
Early on, I decided to title the book using a spin-off of the University of Chicago motto, which can be loosely translated as "Let knowledge grow from more to more; and so be human life enriched." As I was documenting the graffiti, I felt my own life was enriched by graffiti "growing from more to more" on the library walls, and I wanted to convey that in the book title. Unfortunately, I soon discovered that commonly cited "Latin" words for graffiti were all back-formations from Italian. Seeing as there was no attested Latin word for graffiti, and I felt like a paraphrase ("writing on the wall") would make the title too long, I settled for using the English word.

I wrote one of these, or know who wrote one!
Please get in touch! I included in the thanks & acknowledgments section the graffiti artists I've heard from before December 2009. I'd love to hear the story behind the graffiti you wrote and share it on the blog, with your permission.

Where's the rest of the graffiti?
You can find all of the graffiti photographs, organized thematically, on the companion website: http://www.crescatgraffiti.com/graffiti

Have you ever written on the Regenstein walls?
No, though the first piece of graffiti on page 48 really made me want to write something encouraging. I doodled the cover art on a wall in my apartment.

Did you get this idea from the 2004 Scav Hunt item #80: "Brain Farts: The Collected Works of the University of Chicago Bathroom Graffiti"?
I never did (or followed) Scav Hunt as an undergrad, and only heard about that item in a Chicago Weekly blog post[1] about my graffiti project. For what it's worth, none of the graffiti here is from the bathrooms, but anyone interested in UofC graffiti really should check out Michael "mitcho" Erlewine's PDF of the Pierce team's submission, linked from the Chicago Weekly post. The "grout work" is a classic.

[1] http://blog.chicagoweekly.net/2009/10/21/graffiti-at-the-university-of-chicago/

About the Author

Quinn Dombrowski moved into the Max Palevsky dormitory as a first-year in 2002. She spent her first two months of college in the avoiding her room-mates on the 5th floor reading room of the Regenstein Library before throwing all her worldly possessions in a shopping cart, pushing it across Hyde Park, and moving into a friend's closet in the Shoreland until she was re-assigned to that building. She spent the winter of her third year studying for her MA exams on the northwest side of the 4th floor stacks, and received a joint BA/MA in Slavic Linguistics in 2006. After graduation, she chose to pursue a career in academic technologies and currently works at the University of Chicago.

Quinn is married to fellow alumnus Andy Dombrowski, a PhD student in the Department of Slavic Languages and Literatures and the Department of Linguistics. They live in Hyde Park with their two cats, 20 plants, 3,000 books, and the tens of thousands of photographs Quinn takes of random beauty.

You can find Quinn on-line at quinndombrowski.com.

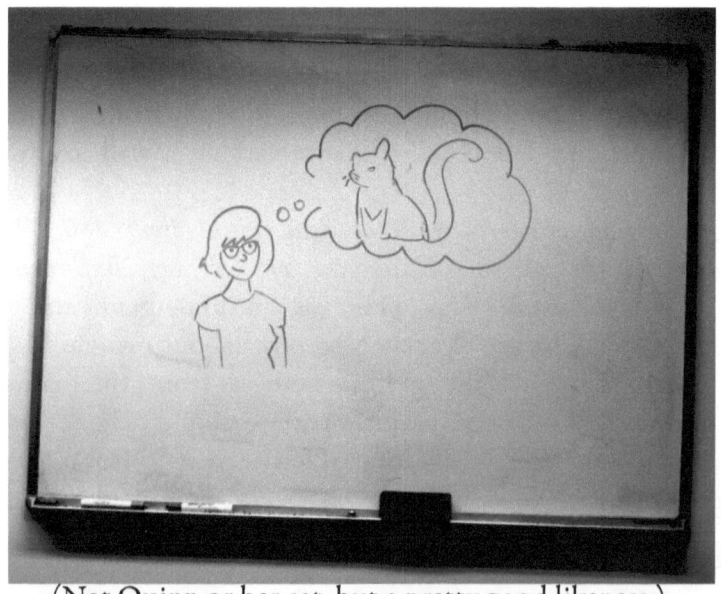

(Not Quinn or her cat, but a pretty good likeness.)

Study as if you'll live forever,
live as if you'll die tomorrow

www.ingramcontent.com/pod-product-compliance
Lightning Source LLC
Chambersburg PA
CBHW030815180526
45163CB00003B/1296